CCEA GCSE CHEMISTRY QUESTIONS

Alyn G McFarland

COLOURPOINT EDUCATIONAL

© Alyn McFarland and Colourpoint Creative Ltd 2019

ISBN: 978 1 78073 189 6

First Edition
Second Impression, 2022

Layout and design: April Sky Design
Printed by: GPS Colour Graphics, Belfast

All rights reserved. No part of this publication may be reproduced, stored in a retrieval system or transmitted in any form or by any means, electronic, mechanical, photocopying, scanning, recording or otherwise, without the prior written permission of the copyright owners and publisher of this book.

Copyright has been acknowledged to the best of our ability. If there are any inadvertent errors or omissions, we shall be happy to correct them in any future editions.

Colourpoint Educational
An imprint of Colourpoint Creative Ltd
Colourpoint House
Jubilee Business Park
21 Jubilee Road
Newtownards
County Down
Northern Ireland
BT23 4YH

Tel: 028 9182 0505
E-mail: sales@colourpoint.co.uk
Web site: www.colourpoint.co.uk

The Author

Dr Alyn G McFarland has been teaching GCSE and GCE A-level Chemistry for 26 years and was Head of Chemistry in a large grammar school for 14 years. He has been writing textbooks, revision guides and workbooks for GCSE Chemistry and GCE A-level Chemistry for different examination boards for over 10 years. Dr McFarland is a senior examiner at both levels for an examination board and also contributes to the PGCE course for Science/Chemistry students on a part-time basis.

Publisher's Note: This book has been written to help students preparing for the GCSE Chemistry specification from CCEA. While Colourpoint Educational and the author have taken every care in its production, we are not able to guarantee that the book is completely error-free. Additionally, while the book has been written to closely match the CCEA specification, it is the responsibility of each candidate to satisfy themselves that they have fully met the requirements of the CCEA specification prior to sitting an exam set by that body. For this reason, and because specifications change with time, we strongly advise every candidate to avail of a qualified teacher and to check the contents of the most recent specification for themselves prior to the exam. Colourpoint Creative Ltd therefore cannot be held responsible for any errors or omissions in this book or any consequences thereof.

Health and Safety: This book describes practical tasks or experiments that are either useful or required for the course. These must only be carried out in a school setting under the supervision of a qualified teacher. It is the responsibility of the school to ensure that students are provided with a safe environment in which to carry out the work. Where it is appropriate, they should consider reference to CLEAPPS.

CONTENTS

Unit 1
Structures, Trends, Chemical Reactions, Quantitative Chemistry and Analysis

1.1	Atomic Structure	5
1.2	Bonding and 1.3 Structures	8
1.4	Nanoparticles	12
1.5	Symbols, Formulae and Equations	14
1.6	The Periodic Table	17
1.7	Quantitative Chemistry	21
1.8	Acids, Bases and Salts	32
1.9	Chemical Analysis	38
1.10	Solubility	44

Unit 2
Further Chemical Reactions, Rates and Equilibrium, Calculations and Organic Chemistry

2.1	Metals and Reactivity Series	49
2.2	Redox, Rusting and Iron	52
2.3	Rates of Reaction	55
2.4	Equilibrium	61
2.5	Organic Chemistry	64
2.6	Quantitative Chemistry	72
2.7	Electrochemistry	81
2.8	Energy Changes in Chemistry	86
2.9	Gas Chemistry	91

Note: This book is designed to be used by both Double Award Chemistry candidates and GCSE Chemistry candidates. Questions that should NOT be attempted by Double Award Chemistry candidates are indicated with grey shading, as shown here, or otherwise indicated in the text.

Note: The answers for this book are available online. Visit www.colourpointeducational.com and search for *Chemistry Questions for CCEA GCSE*. The page for this book will contain instructions for downloading the mark scheme. If you have any difficulties please contact Colourpoint – details on the previous page.

Unit 1
Structures, Trends, Chemical Reactions, Quantitative Chemistry and Analysis

1.1 Atomic Structure

1. Complete the table below.

Subatomic particle	Relative charge	Relative mass
		$\frac{1}{1840}$
	+1	
neutron		

[3]

2. The diagrams below show two different models of the atom.

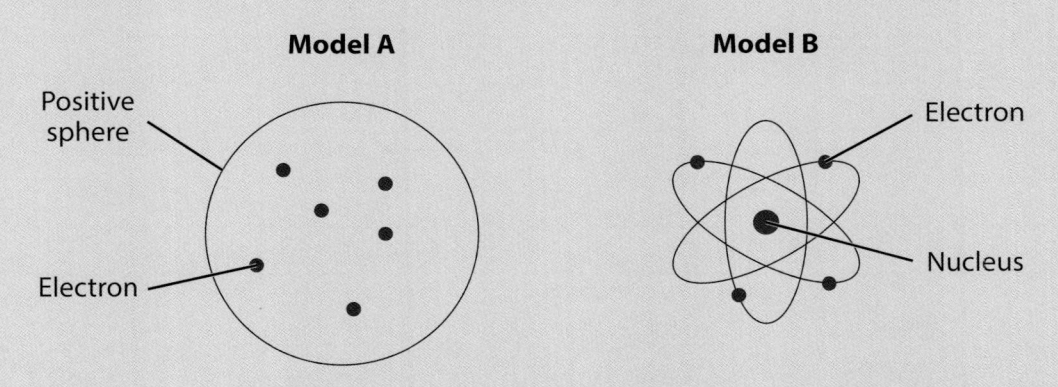

Model A — Positive sphere, Electron

Model B — Electron, Nucleus

   (a) What name is used for Model A? [1]
   (b) Name the scientist who developed Model B. [1]
   (c) The neutron is missing from Model B. Suggest why it was discovered later than the other subatomic particles. [1]

3. The table below gives details of some atoms and ions.

Particle	Atomic number	Electronic configuration
A	7	2, 5
B	16	2, 8, 8
C	3	2
D	12	2, 8
E	9	2, 7

   (a) Which particles (A, B, C, D or E) are atoms? [1]
   (b) Which particle (A, B, C, D or E) is of an element in Group 5? [1]
   (c) Write the formula of particle C including any charge. [1]
   (d) Which particle (A, B, C, D or E) has a charge of 2–? [1]

5

STRUCTURES, TRENDS, CHEMICAL REACTIONS, QUANTITATIVE CHEMISTRY AND ANALYSIS

4. The atomic radius of a gallium atom is 1.87×10^{-10} m. The nuclear radius is 36 300 times smaller than the atomic radius. Calculate the nuclear radius to 3 significant figures in femtometres (fm). 1 fm = 1×10^{-15} m [2]

5. An atom of an element has 21 protons, 18 electrons and 24 neutrons.
   (a) Identify the element. [1]
   (b) What is the charge on the ion of the element? [1]
   (c) What is the mass number of the element? [1]
   (d) What is the electronic configuration of the ion? [1]
   (e) Write the formulae of two other ions, including the charge, which have the same electronic configuration. [1]

6. Complete the table below for some simple atoms and ions.

Atom/Ion	Atomic Number	Mass Number	Number of protons	Number of neutrons	Number of electrons	Electronic Configuration
Be	4	9			4	
Cl⁻			17	20	18	
	19	39				2, 8, 8
	10			10	10	
Mg²⁺		24	12			
	7	14				2, 8

[6]

7. (a) Hydrogen (atomic number 1) has three isotopes with mass numbers 1, 2 and 3.
   (i) What is meant by the term isotopes? [2]
   (ii) Draw a labelled diagram of an atom of hydrogen with mass number 3, showing the location and number of all the subatomic particles. [2]

   (b) An isotope of another element has 5 protons and 6 neutrons.
   (i) Identify the element. [1]
   (ii) What is the mass number of this isotope? [1]
   (iii) Write the electronic configuration of an atom of this isotope. [1]

   (c) Sulfur has three isotopes, as shown in the table below.

Isotope	Relative abundance
³²S	95.0
³³S	0.75
³⁴S	4.25

   (i) Calculate the relative atomic mass of sulfur. Give your answer to 1 decimal place. Show your working out. [3]
   (ii) Explain why isotopes have the same chemical properties. [1]

1.1 ATOMIC STRUCTURE

8. The diagram below show the electronic configuration of several atoms and ions. They are labelled **U** to **Z**. The letters do not represent symbols for the elements.

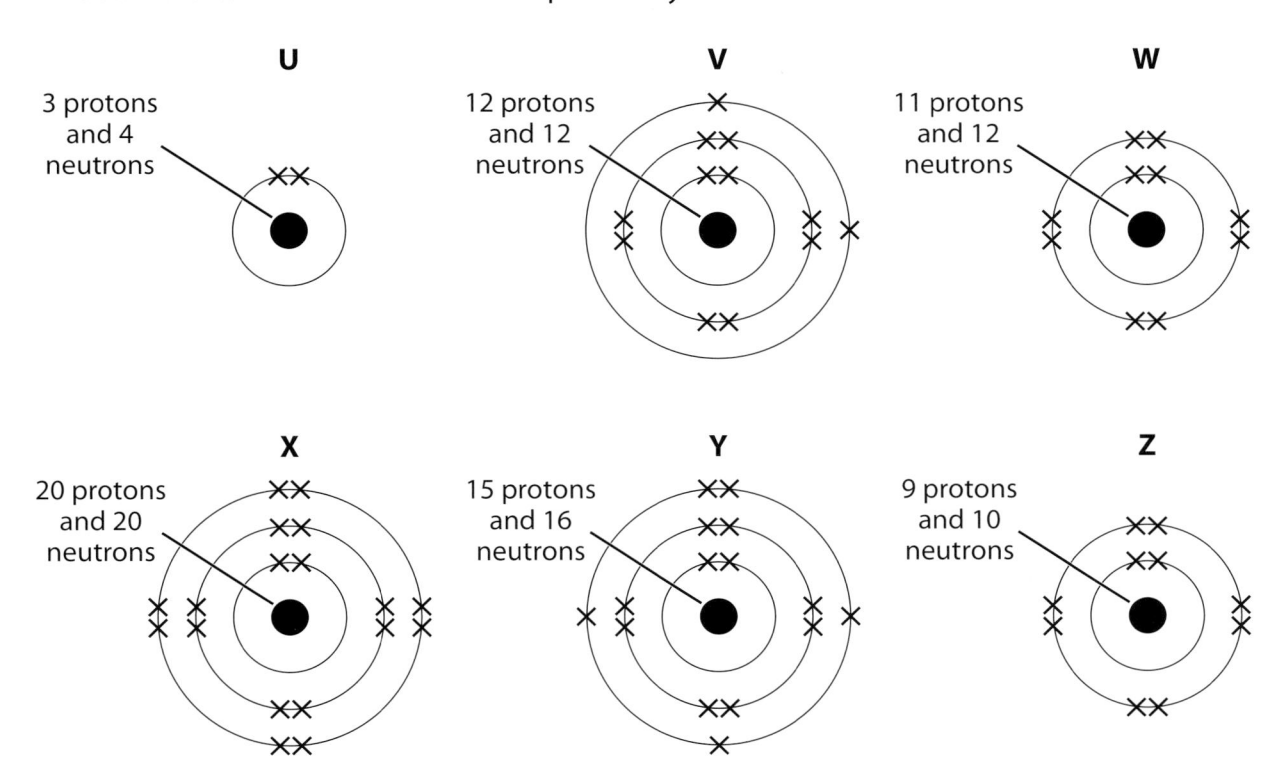

U: 3 protons and 4 neutrons
V: 12 protons and 12 neutrons
W: 11 protons and 12 neutrons
X: 20 protons and 20 neutrons
Y: 15 protons and 16 neutrons
Z: 9 protons and 10 neutrons

(a) Complete the table below giving the identity of the atom or ion (including any charge on the ion) and the atomic number, mass number and electronic configuration of **A** to **F**.

Atom/Ion	Identity	Atomic number	Mass number	Number of electrons	Electronic configuration
U	Li$^+$				
V					2, 8, 2
W				10	
X		20			
Y				15	
Z			19		

[5]

(b) Which **two** of the atoms or ions (**U**, **V**, **W**, **X**, **Y** and **Z**) above are from elements in the same group of the Periodic Table? [1]

(c) Explain why atoms are electrically neutral. [1]

(d) Draw a labelled diagram of an oxide ion which has a mass number of 16, showing the charge on the ion and the location and number of all the subatomic particles. [3]

1.2 Bonding and 1.3 Structures

1. The table below shows some ions labelled **A** to **I**.

A	B	C	D	E	F	G	H	I
CO_3^{2-}	K^+	Al^{3+}	NO_3^-	O^{2-}	SO_4^{2-}	Cu^{2+}	NH_4^+	Br^-

   (a) Use the letters **A** to **I** to answers the questions.
   - (i) Which, if any, are anions? [1]
   - (ii) Which, if any, are both molecular ions and cations? [1]

   (b) Name all the ions **A** to **I**. [9]

   (c) Write the formula of the compound formed between the following ions:
   - (i) **A** and **B** [1]
   - (ii) **C** and **E** [1]
   - (iii) **D** and **G** [1]

2. Sodium oxide is an ionic compound. It has a melting point of 1132 °C.
   - (a) Write the formula for sodium oxide. [1]
   - (b) Show, using a dot and cross diagram, how atoms of sodium react with atoms of oxygen to form sodium oxide. Include the charges on the ions formed. [6]
   - (c) Explain why sodium oxide has a high melting point. [2]
   - (d) State **two** other physical properties of sodium oxide. [2]
   - (e) From the compounds shown below, circle any other ionic compounds.

   lithium iodide   hydrogen chloride   ammonium chloride   water

   hydrogen sulfide   carbon dioxide   magnesium oxide   sodium sulfate

   [2]
   - (f) Ionic compounds contain ionic bonding. What is meant by ionic bonding? [2]
   - (g) What is the structure of sodium oxide? [1]

1.2 BONDING AND 1.3 STRUCTURES

3. Complete the table below. The first row has been completed for you.

Name of compound	Formula of compound	Formula of positive ion	Formula of negative ion
sodium chloride	NaCl	Na⁺	Cl⁻
		Mg²⁺	O²⁻
	AlF₃		
	KNO₃		
calcium sulfate			
copper(II) hydroxide			
		Zn²⁺	Br⁻
iron(III) oxide			

[8]

4. Methane reacts with oxygen to form carbon dioxide and water.
 (a) Write a balanced symbol equation for the reaction. [3]
 (b) Draw a dot and cross diagram for methane. [1]
 (c) The dot and cross diagram for an oxygen molecule is shown below.

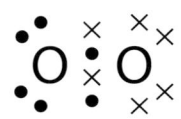

 (i) Label any lone pair of electrons on the diagram. [1]
 (ii) Name the type of bonding found in an oxygen molecule. [1]
 (iii) Name the type of bonding found between oxygen molecules. [1]
 (iv) Explain why the bonding in an oxygen molecule is often shown as O=O. [2]
 (v) Oxygen is a diatomic element. What is meant by the term diatomic? [1]

 (d) Draw a dot and cross diagram for water. [1]
 (e) How many lone pairs are present in a molecule of carbon dioxide? [1]

STRUCTURES, TRENDS, CHEMICAL REACTIONS, QUANTITATIVE CHEMISTRY AND ANALYSIS

5. Ammonia is a compound formed from nitrogen and hydrogen. The equation below shows the molecules involved in the reaction. A very high temperature is required to break the bonds in the nitrogen molecule. Nitrogen, hydrogen and ammonia are all gases at room temperature and pressure.

$$N \equiv N \;+\; 3\,H-H \;\rightarrow\; 2\,H-\underset{H}{\overset{N}{\underset{|}{}}}-H$$

(a) Name the type of bonding found in all three molecules. [1]
(b) Explain why a very high temperature is required to break the bonds in the nitrogen molecule. [2]
(c) Draw a dot and cross diagram for all three molecules. Label all lone pairs of electrons. [4]
(d) Explain why ammonia is a gas at room temperature and pressure. [2]
(e) Write a balanced symbol equation for the reaction. [1]
(f) Ammonia reacts with hydrochloric acid to form ammonium chloride.
  (i) Write a balanced symbol equation for this reaction. [2]
  (ii) Explain why ammonium chloride is a solid at room temperature. [2]

6. The table below gives information on four substances.

Substance	Melting point (°C)	Boiling point (°C)	Electrical conduction when solid	Electrical conduction when molten
Iron	1500	2862	good	good
Sodium oxide	1132	1950	poor	good
Chlorine	−102	−34	poor	poor
Silicon dioxide	1710	2230	poor	poor

(a) Explain why iron has a high melting point. [2]
(b) Explain why iron conducts electricity. [2]
(c) State the type of bonding present in sodium oxide. [1]
(d) Explain why sodium oxide conducts electricity when molten. [2]
(e) State the type of bonding found in chlorine molecules. [1]
(f) Explain why chlorine has a low melting point. [2]
(g) State the structure of chlorine. [1]
(h) Give two pieces of evidence to explain why silicon dioxide is giant covalent. [2]

1.2 BONDING AND 1.3 STRUCTURES

7. Carbon exists as several allotropes including graphite and graphene.
   (a) Graphite is a slippery dark grey solid which conducts electricity.
      (i) Draw a labelled diagram to show the structure and bonding in graphite. [4]
      (ii) Explain why graphite conducts electricity. [2]
      (iii) State one other property of graphite. [1]

   (b) Two other allotropes of carbon are shown below.

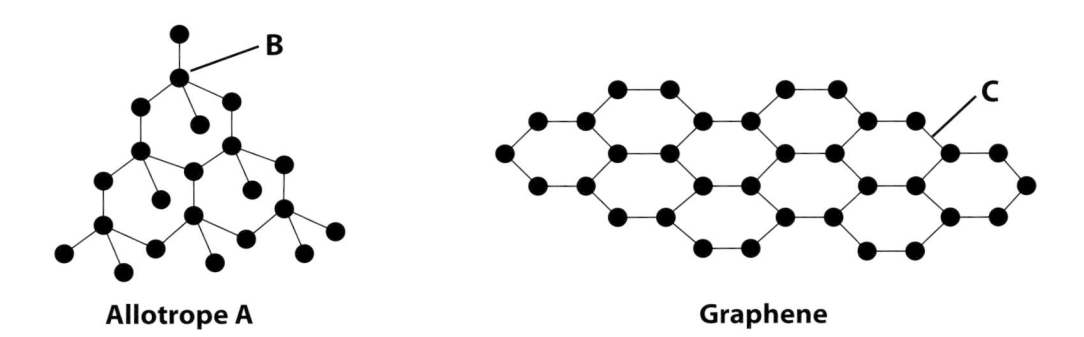

   Allotrope A   **Graphene**

   (i) Name allotrope A. [1]
   (ii) What is represented by the black dot labelled B? [1]
   (iii) What is represented by the line labelled C? [1]
   (iv) What is meant by the term allotrope? [2]
   (v) State one use of graphene. [1]

8. Sodium and magnesium are typical metals.
   (a) Draw a labelled diagram to show the structure and bonding in sodium metal. [3]
   (b) Explain why metals conduct electricity and suggest why magnesium is a better electrical conductor than sodium. [3]
   (c) The alloy duralumin is used to make aircraft bodies. It is composed of 95% aluminium and 4.5% copper. The remaining 0.5% is made up of magnesium and other metals as well as silicon.
      (i) What is meant by the term alloy? [3]
      (ii) Explain why duralumin is harder than aluminium on its own. [2]
      (iii) Suggest one reason why duralumin is used to make aircraft bodies. [1]

9. Gold purity is measured in carats. The table below shows some different carat rated gold. Complete the table.

Carat rating	Percentage of pure gold (%)
24	
	75
11	

[3]

1.4 Nanoparticles

1. Nanoparticles contain only a few hundred atoms and they are 1 – 100 nm in size. Zinc oxide nanoparticles are used in some sun creams instead of bulk zinc oxide particles.
   (a) What is a nanometre? [1]
   (b) Explain why some people have reservations about the use of nanoparticles. [1]
   (c) State one advantage of using zinc oxide nanoparticles rather than bulk particles in sun creams. [1]

2. Two cubes are shown below. Cube A has a side length of 1 mm whereas cube B has a side length of 20 mm.

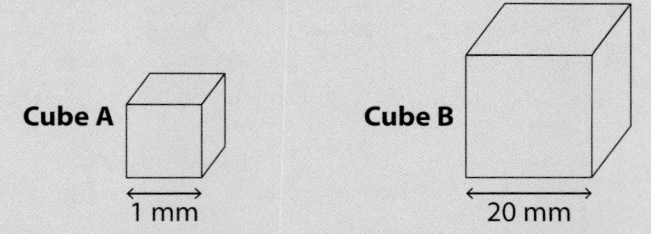

   Cube A
   1 mm

   Cube B
   20 mm

   (a) Complete the table below by calculating the surface area and volume of the two cubes and the surface area to volume ratio using the expression given below

   $$\text{Surface area to volume ratio} = \frac{\text{surface area (mm}^2\text{)}}{\text{volume (mm}^3\text{)}}$$

	Cube A	Cube B
Surface area (mm^2)		
Volume (mm^3)		
Surface area to volume ratio		

   [6]

   (b) Convert 20 mm to nanometres. [1]
   (c) What is the effect on surface area to volume ratio of increasing the side length of cube by a factor of 20, as in the example above? [1]

3. A cube has a surface area to volume ratio of 6:15 or 0.4. The surface area of the cube is 1350 nm^2.
   (a) Calculate the volume of the cube and state the units. [2]
   (b) Calculate the length of one side of the cube in nm. [2]
   (c) Calculate the length of one side of the cube in m. [1]

1.4 NANOPARTICLES

4. The table below gives information about three different cubes, X, Y and Z.

	Cube X	Cube Y	Cube Z
Side length	4 cm		
Surface area			150 nm^2
Volume		512 mm^3	
Surface area to volume ratio			

Complete the table. [9]

1.5 Symbols, Formulae and Equations

1. Some elements and compounds are shown below.

oxygen	methane	sodium sulfate	sulfur	argon
copper(II) hydroxide	nitrogen	magnesium oxide	ammonia	water

   (a) Which elements, if any, from the list above are diatomic? [1]
   (b) Which compounds, if any, from the list above contain only two elements? [1]
   (c) Write the formulae of the compounds: copper(II) hydroxide, sodium sulfate, methane and ammonia. [4]
   (d) Write a balanced symbol equation for the reaction of magnesium with oxygen to form magnesium oxide. [3]

2. Write the formula of the following compounds.
   (a) potassium bromide [1]
   (b) calcium oxide [1]
   (c) magnesium chloride [1]
   (d) iron(II) hydroxide [1]
   (e) aluminium sulfate [1]
   (f) chromium(III) nitrate [1]
   (g) ammonium sulfate [1]

3. Name the following compounds.
   (a) ZnO [1]
   (b) $AgNO_3$ [1]
   (c) K_2CO_3 [1]
   (d) $Fe(NO_3)_2$ [1]
   (e) $Ca(HCO_3)_2$ [1]
   (f) $CuSO_4$ [1]
   (g) $Al(OH)_3$ [1]

4. Write balanced symbol equations for the following reactions.
   (a) iron + sulfur → iron(II) sulfide [2]
   (b) zinc + steam → zinc oxide + hydrogen [2]
       Hint: steam has the same formula as water.
   (c) copper + oxygen → copper(II) oxide [3]
   (d) aluminium + oxygen → aluminium oxide [3]
   (e) hydrogen + chlorine → hydrogen chloride [3]
   (f) aluminium oxide + hydrochloric acid → aluminium chloride + water [3]
   (g) lithium + oxygen → lithium oxide [3]
   (h) potassium + water → potassium hydroxide + hydrogen [3]

5. Write balanced symbol equations for the following reactions.
   (a) sodium hydroxide + hydrochloric acid → sodium chloride + water [2]
   (b) copper(II) hydroxide + nitric acid → copper(II) nitrate + water [3]

1.5 SYMBOLS, FORMULAE AND EQUATIONS

    (c) potassium hydrogencarbonate + sulfuric acid → potassium sulfate + carbon dioxide + water [3]
    (d) ammonia + hydrochloric acid → ammonium chloride [2]
    (e) aluminium hydroxide + sulfuric acid → aluminium sulfate + water [3]
    (f) magnesium + nitric acid → magnesium nitrate + hydrogen [3]
    (g) ammonium sulfate + sodium hydroxide → sodium sulfate + ammonia + water [3]

6. (a) Calcium hydroxide solution reacts with carbon dioxide gas for form solid calcium carbonate and water.
Write a balanced symbol equation for the reaction including state symbols. [3]
  (b) Silver nitrate solution was added to a solution of lithium bromide and the products were solid silver bromide and lithium nitrate solution.
    (i) Write a balanced symbol equation for this reaction including state symbols. [3]
    (ii) Write an ionic equation for the reaction including state symbols. [3]

7. The following general reactions should be used to help you answer the questions which follow.

Reaction	General Equation
1	metal/non-metal + oxygen → metal/non-metal oxide
2	metal + water → metal hydroxide + hydrogen
3	metal + steam → metal oxide + hydrogen
4	metal + acid → metal salt + hydrogen
5	metal oxide + acid → metal salt + water
6	metal hydroxide + acid → metal salt + water
7	metal carbonate + acid → metal salt + carbon dioxide + water
8	metal hydrogencarbonate + acid → metal salt + carbon dioxide + water
9	ammonia + acid → ammonium salt

The salt name depends on the acid:
- Hydrochloric acid forms a **chloride** salt.
- Sulfuric acid forms a **sulfate** salt.
- Nitric acid forms a **nitrate** salt.

Write balanced symbol equations for the following reactions:
(a) Calcium reacting with oxygen [3]
(b) Zinc reacting with hydrochloric acid [3]
(c) Copper(II) oxide reacting with sulfuric acid [2]
(d) Lithium carbonate reacting with sulfuric acid [2]
(e) Ammonia reacting with sulfuric acid [3]
(f) Iron(III) hydroxide reacting with nitric acid [3]
(g) Sodium hydrogencarbonate reacting with hydrochloric acid [2]
(h) Calcium reacting with water [3]
(i) Magnesium reacting with steam [2]

STRUCTURES, TRENDS, CHEMICAL REACTIONS, QUANTITATIVE CHEMISTRY AND ANALYSIS

8. Zinc reacts with copper(II) sulfate solution according to the balanced symbol equation below:

$$Zn(s) + CuSO_4(aq) \rightarrow ZnSO_4(aq) + Cu(s)$$

(a) Identify the ion which does not take part in this reaction. [1]

(b) Write an ionic equation for the reaction. [2]

(c) Write the two half equations for the reactions which are occurring.
Hint: A half equation shows either the loss or gain of electrons. [6]

1.6 The Periodic Table

1. The table below is a representation of the Periodic system of elements developed by Mendeleev in 1869. The elements were arranged in order of "atomic weights".

hydrogen						
lithium	beryllium	boron	carbon	nitrogen	oxygen	fluorine
sodium	magnesium	aluminium	silicon	phosphorus	sulfur	chlorine
potassium	calcium		**Element X**	arsenic	selenium	bromine
rubidium	zinc					

   (a) Suggest why hydrogen is grouped with Group 1 elements. [1]
   (b) Element X had not been discovered in 1869. Which element took this position in the Periodic Table? [1]
   (c) Suggest why Mendeleev ordered his elements by "atomic weights" rather than atomic number. [1]
   (d) State **two other** features of the Mendeleev's table which are different from the modern Periodic Table. [2]

2. The diagram below is an outline of part of the Periodic Table.

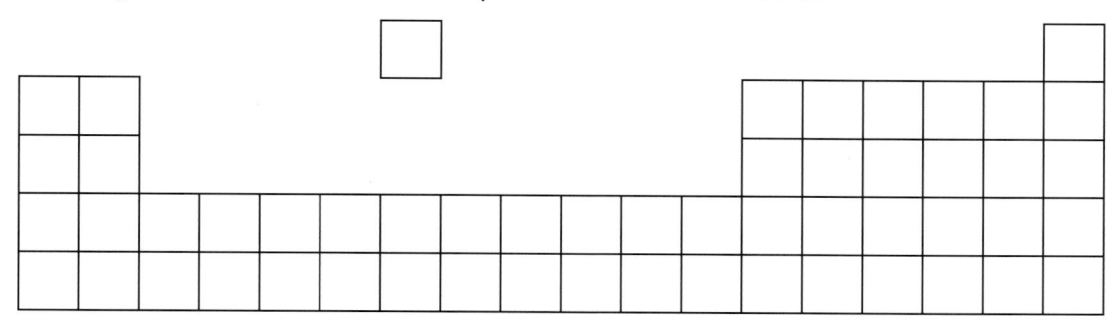

   Using the letters **W**, **X**, **Y** and **Z** show the position of the following elements on the outline of the Periodic Table above based on the description below.

   W is a yellow-green gas.

   X reacts with water producing a lilac flame.

   Y is a liquid non-metal.

   Z is the element in Period 3 and Group 4. [4]

3. Often a short form of the Periodic Table like the one shown below is used.

Group 1	2	3	4	5	6	7	0
H							He
Li	Be	B	C	N	O	F	Ne
Na	Mg	Al	Si	P	S	Cl	Ar
K	Ca	Ga	Ge	As	Se	Br	Kr

(a) Using **ONLY** the elements in the table above:
 (i) Name one noble gas. [1]
 (ii) Name one colourless diatomic gas. [1]
 (iii) Name one non-metal which is a solid at room temperature and pressure. [1]
 (iv) Name one element which forms a simple ion with a charge of 2–. [1]
 (v) Name the most reactive element in Group 7. [1]
 (vi) Name the Group 0 element with the lowest boiling point. [1]
 (vii) Name one element which exists as allotropes. [1]

(b) Explain why the Group 0 elements are unreactive. [1]

4. The Periodic Table lists all known elements. Mendeleev made the most major contribution to its development.
 (a) What is meant by the term element? [1]
 (b) Describe three differences between the modern Periodic Table and the Periodic Table developed by Mendeleev. [3]
 (c) The Periodic Table contains metals and non-metals. Most metals are solids with high melting points and boiling points. State two other physical properties of metals. [2]
 (d) Complete the table below.

Group of the Periodic Table	Name of group
1	
2	
7	

[3]
 (e) Explain why elements in the same group have similar chemical properties. [1]

1.6 THE PERIODIC TABLE

5. Group 1 elements are very reactive.
   (a) State how sodium is stored and explain why it is stored in this way. [2]
   (b) Circle the observations below to describe what you would observe when sodium reacts with water.

floats	sinks then rises	lilac flame	melts to form a silvery ball
disappears	colourless solution formed	white solid formed	heat released

   [2]

   (c) Write a balanced symbol equation for sodium reacting with water. [3]
   (d) When sodium reacts with water, a sodium atom becomes a sodium ion.
      (i) Write a half equation for this reaction. [2]
      (ii) What is the electronic configuration of a sodium ion? [1]

   (e) Explain in terms of reactivity and electrons why the reaction of potassium with water is more vigorous than the reaction of sodium with water. [3]

6. A piece of potassium was removed from its storage jar, a small piece was cut using a scalpel and patted using filter paper before adding it to a large volume of water behind a safety screen.
   (a) Describe the appearance of the potassium when freshly cut and a few minutes after being cut. [2]
   (b) Explain why the potassium was cut into a small piece. [1]
   (c) Why was the potassium patted using filter paper? [1]
   (d) Why was a large volume of water used? [1]
   (e) Why was the reaction carried out behind a safety screen? [1]
   (f) Name the products of the reaction of potassium with water. [2]
   (g) Explain whether potassium is less dense or denser than water based on the observations made during the reaction. [1]

7. Group 7 elements are reactive non-metals.
   (a) Describe the appearance of each of the halogens (fluorine, chlorine, bromine and iodine) including colour and state at room temperature and pressure. [4]
   (b) Chlorine gas reacts with potassium iodide solution. The solution changes colour as chlorine is bubbled into it.
      (i) Write a balanced symbol equation for this reaction. [3]
      (ii) State the type of reaction which is occurring. [1]
      (iii) What colour change is observed in the solution during this reaction? [2]
      (iv) Write an ionic equation for the reaction. [3]
      (v) Write two half equations for the processes occurring in this reaction. [6]

8. Bromine water is added to a solution of sodium iodide and a reaction occurs.
   (a) Explain why the colour change in this reaction is not very noticeable. [2]
   (b) Write a balanced symbol equation for the reaction. [3]
   (c) Explain, in terms of electrons, why bromine is more reactive than iodine. [2]

9. **(a)** Chlorine gas may be produced by passing an electric current through a concentrated solution of sodium chloride called brine. Chloride ions in the brine lose electrons to become chlorine molecules.
   - **(i)** Describe how you would test for chlorine gas. [2]
   - **(ii)** Write a half equation for the conversion of chloride ions into a chlorine molecule. [3]
   - **(iii)** Suggest why it requires more electrical energy to remove electrons from chloride ions than it does to remove electrons from iodide ions. [2]

   (b) Iodine changes directly from a solid to a gas when heated.
   - **(i)** What name is used for this change of state? [1]
   - **(ii)** What is observed when solid iodine is heated? [2]

10. Describe the displacement reactions which occur between chlorine and solutions of sodium bromide and sodium iodide. Your answer should include:
    - balanced symbol equations for the reactions,
    - an explanation of why the reactions occur in terms of reactivity, and
    - the colour changes observed in the solutions during the reaction.

    In this question, you will be assessed on the quality of your written communication including the use of specialist scientific terms. [6]

11. Transition metals have similar physical properties to Group 1 metals but different chemical properties.

    (a) Describe how the melting points of the transition metals differ from the melting points of the Group 1 metals. [1]

    (b) Complete the table below giving the colour of the solid compounds and the solutions.

Substance	Colour
potassium iodide solution	
solid copper(II) oxide	
copper(II) sulfate solution	
solid sodium bromide	
solid copper(II) carbonate	
hydrated copper(II) sulfate	

    [6]

1.7 Quantitative Chemistry

Basics of Quantitative Chemistry

1. Complete the paragraph below using the items in the box.

atomic numbers	atom	carbon–12
sodium–23	mass numbers	weighted
hydrogen–1	12	1/12
average	1	isotope

The relative atomic mass is the mass of an _____ compared with that of the

_____ isotope, which has a mass of exactly _____. The relative

atomic mass is the _____ mean of the _____. [5]

2. Complete the table below.

Name of compound	Formula of compound	Relative formula mass (M_r)
	H_2O	
calcium bromide		
aluminium nitrate		
potassium nitrate		
	Fe_2O_3	
chromium(III) sulfate		
ammonium carbonate		
copper(II) carbonate		
magnesium hydroxide		
zinc sulfate-7-water		
silver(I) nitrate		
sodium carbonate		

[12]

STRUCTURES, TRENDS, CHEMICAL REACTIONS, QUANTITATIVE CHEMISTRY AND ANALYSIS

Interchanging mass and moles

3. Determine the number of moles in the following:
   (a) 2.7 g of Al [1]
   (b) 32.1 g of NH_4Cl [1]
   (c) 144 g of $Fe(NO_3)_2$ [1]
   (d) 17.76 g of Li_2CO_3 [1]
   (e) 6.48 g of $Ca(HCO_3)_2$ [1]

4. Determine the mass of the following number of moles:
   (a) 0.075 moles of $Ca(NO_3)_2$ [1]
   (b) 0.04 moles of $CoCl_2.6H_2O$ [1]
   (c) 1.75 moles of TiO_2 [1]
   (d) 0.5 moles of Al_2O_3 [1]
   (e) 0.04 moles of $CuSO_4.5H_2O$ [1]

5. Calculate the following:
   (a) The number of moles in 4.2 kg of $MgCO_3$ [2]
   (b) The mass, in kg, in 120 moles of $NaNO_3$ [2]
   (c) The number of moles in 11.2 tonnes of Fe_2O_3 [2]
   (d) The mass, in tonnes, in 40000 moles of $NaHCO_3$ [2]
   (e) The number of moles in 19.5 kg of $Al(OH)_3$ [2]
   (f) The mass, in kg, in 200 moles of hydrated sodium carbonate, $Na_2CO_3.10H_2O$ [2]

Reacting mass calculations

6. Lithium reacts with oxygen to form lithium oxide.

   $$4Li + O_2 \rightarrow 2Li_2O$$

   Calculate the mass of lithium oxide formed when 1.75 g of lithium reacts completely with oxygen. [3]

7. Calculate the mass of silver produced when 4.76 g of silver nitrate, $AgNO_3$, are heated to constant mass.

   $$2AgNO_3 \rightarrow 2Ag + 2NO_2 + O_2$$
   [3]

8. Calcium nitride reacts with water according to the equation:

   $$Ca_3N_2 + 6H_2O \rightarrow 3Ca(OH)_2 + 2NH_3$$

   Calculate the mass of calcium hydroxide formed when 8.14 g of calcium nitride reacts with excess water. [3]

9. Calculate the mass, in kg, of iron(III) oxide, Fe_2O_3, which would be required to produce 560 kg of iron in the blast furnace.

   $$Fe_2O_3 + 3CO \rightarrow 2Fe + 3CO_2$$
   [4]

1.7 QUANTITATIVE CHEMISTRY

10. Sodium thiosulfate, $Na_2S_2O_3$ decomposes on heating according to the equation:

$$4Na_2S_2O_3 \rightarrow 3Na_2SO_4 + Na_2S_5$$

Calculate the mass of Na_2SO_4 formed when 711 g of sodium thiosulfate are heated to constant mass. [3]

11. Calculate the mass of sodium carbonate formed when 6.72 g of sodium hydrogencarbonate are heated to constant mass.

$$2NaHCO_3 \rightarrow Na_2CO_3 + CO_2 + H_2O$$

[3]

12. Calculate the mass of aluminium required to react with excess oxygen to form 4.59 g of aluminium oxide.

$$4Al + 3O_2 \rightarrow 2Al_2O_3$$

[3]

13. Calculate the mass of iron(III) hydroxide which would be required to form 432 g of iron(III) oxide.

$$2Fe(OH)_3 \rightarrow Fe_2O_3 + 3H_2O$$

[3]

14. Calculate the mass of Fe_3O_4 formed when 2.24 g of iron are reacted with excess steam. Give your answer to 1 decimal place.

$$3Fe(s) + 4H_2O(g) \rightarrow Fe_3O_4(s) + 4H_2(g)$$

[3]

15. Lead(II) nitrate, $Pb(NO_3)_2$ decomposes when heated according to the equation:

$$2Pb(NO_3)_2(s) \rightarrow 2PbO(s) + 4NO_2(g) + O_2(g)$$

Calculate the loss in mass which would observed on heating 3.31 g of lead(II) nitrate, $Pb(NO_3)_2$, to constant mass. [4]

Limiting reactant calculations

16. Calculate the mass, in g, of zinc chloride formed when 0.12 moles of zinc are reacted with 0.25 moles of hydrochloric acid, where one reactant is the limiting reactant.

$$Zn + 2HCl \rightarrow ZnCl_2 + H_2$$

[3]

17. Calculate the mass (in g) of sulfur trioxide formed when 1.5 moles of sulfur dioxide reacts with 0.6 moles of oxygen, where one reactant is the limiting reactant.

$$2SO_2 + O_2 \rightarrow 2SO_3$$

[3]

STRUCTURES, TRENDS, CHEMICAL REACTIONS, QUANTITATIVE CHEMISTRY AND ANALYSIS

18. Ammonium sulfate reacts with sodium hydroxide according to the equation:

$$(NH_4)_2SO_4(s) + 2NaOH(s) \rightarrow Na_2SO_4(s) + 2H_2O(l) + 2NH_3(g)$$

2.64 g of $(NH_4)_2SO_4$ were reacted with 1.40 g of sodium hydroxide.

(a) Calculate the number of moles of $(NH_4)_2SO_4$ used. [1]
(b) Calculate the number of moles of NaOH used. [1]
(c) Determine which reactant is the limiting reactant. [1]
(d) Calculate the number of moles of Na_2SO_4 formed. [1]
(e) Calculate the mass of Na_2SO_4 formed. [1]

19. Potassium superoxide (KO_2) reacts with carbon dioxide according to the equation:

$$4KO_2(s) + 2CO_2(g) \rightarrow 2K_2CO_3(s) + 3O_2(g)$$

3.55 kg of potassium superoxide were reacted with 968 g of carbon dioxide.

(a) Calculate the number of moles of potassium superoxide used. [2]
(b) Calculate the number of moles of carbon dioxide used. [1]
(c) Determine which reactant is the limiting reactant. [1]
(d) Calculate the number of moles of oxygen formed. [1]
(e) Calculate the mass of oxygen formed in kg. [2]

20. Aluminium oxide reacts with calcium according to the equation:

$$Al_2O_3 + 3Ca \rightarrow 3CaO + 2Al$$

6.12 g of aluminium oxide were reacted with 4.80 g of calcium.

(a) Show, by calculation, that calcium is the limiting reactant. [3]
(b) Calculate the mass of aluminium formed in g. [2]
(c) Calculate the mass of aluminium oxide left over. [2]

21. Lithium reacts with sulfur according to the equation:

$$2Li + S \rightarrow 2Li_2S$$

(a) Calculate the mass of lithium sulfide formed when 2.1 g of lithium reacts with 4.0 g of sulfur. [5]
(b) Calculate the mass of the excess reactant left over. [3]

22. Ammonia reacts with oxygen according to the equation:

$$4NH_3 + 3O_2 \rightarrow 2N_2 + 6H_2O$$

(a) Calculate the mass of nitrogen formed when 13.6 g of ammonia were reacted with 20.0 g of oxygen. [5]
(b) Calculate the mass of the excess reactant left over. [3]

1.7 QUANTITATIVE CHEMISTRY

Percentage yield calculations

23. In an experiment to prepare calcium nitrate from calcium carbonate and nitric acid, the following reaction occurred:

$$CaCO_3 + 2HNO_3 \rightarrow Ca(NO_3)_2 + CO_2 + H_2O$$

14.5 g of calcium carbonate were reacted with excess nitric acid. 20.8 g of calcium nitrate were obtained.

(a) Calculate the theoretical yield of calcium nitrate in grams. [3]
(b) Calculate the percentage yield of calcium nitrate. Give your answer to 1 decimal place. [2]

24. Ammonia reacts with chlorine according to the equation:

$$8NH_3 + 3Cl_2 \rightarrow 6NH_4Cl + N_2$$

6.8 kg of ammonia were reacted with excess chlorine.
7.0 kg of ammonium chloride were obtained.

(a) Calculate the theoretical yield of ammonium chloride in kg. [4]
(b) Calculate the percentage yield of ammonium chloride. Give your answer to 1 decimal place. [2]

25. Vanadium metal may be obtained from vanadium(V) oxide, V_2O_5, by reaction with calcium or aluminium. The word equations are shown below:

vanadium(V) oxide + calcium → calcium oxide + vanadium

vanadium(V) oxide + aluminium → aluminium oxide + vanadium

(a) Write a balanced symbol equation for the reaction of vanadium(V) oxide with calcium. [3]
(b) 8.19 tonnes of vanadium(V) oxide were reacted with excess aluminium. The balanced symbol equation for the reaction is given below. 3.80 tonnes of vanadium were obtained.

$$3V_2O_5 + 10Al \rightarrow 5Al_2O_3 + 6V$$

　(i) Calculate the theoretical yield of vanadium in tonnes. [4]
　(ii) Calculate the percentage yield of vanadium. Give your answer to 2 decimal places.
　(iii) Suggest **one** reason why the percentage yield is not 100%. [1]

STRUCTURES, TRENDS, CHEMICAL REACTIONS, QUANTITATIVE CHEMISTRY AND ANALYSIS

26. 20.8 g of hydrated copper(II) sulfate, $CuSO_4.5H_2O$ were obtained during a salt preparation using 12.4 g of copper(II) carbonate and sulfuric acid. The method is shown in the flow scheme below.

Add excess copper(II) carbonate to 25 cm³ of sulfuric acid in a conical flask → Filter off the excess copper(II) carbonate → Heat the filtrate to evaporate to half volume → Allow the filtrate to cool and crystallise → Filter off the crystals of hydrated copper(II) sulfate and dry in a desiccator

The equation for the reaction is:

$$CuCO_3(s) + H_2SO_4(aq) \rightarrow CuSO_4(aq) + CO_2(g) + H_2O(l)$$

(a) Calculate the number of moles of copper(II) carbonate used. [1]
(b) Calculate the maximum number of moles of $CuSO_4(aq)$ formed. [1]
(c) Assuming every mole of $CuSO_4(aq)$ forms $CuSO_4.5H_2O$, calculate the maximum mass of $CuSO_4.5H_2O$ which could be formed. [1]
(d) Calculate the percentage yield. [2]
(e) Using the practical information in the flow scheme, suggest two practical reasons why the percentage yield was not 100%. [2]

27. Sodium hydroxide solution was added to a solution of iron(III) chloride. A precipitate of iron(III) hydroxide formed. The equation for the reaction is:

$$3NaOH(aq) + FeCl_3(aq) \rightarrow Fe(OH)_3(s) + 3NaCl(aq)$$

The solution of sodium hydroxide contained 12.0 g of sodium hydroxide and the solution of iron(III) chloride contained 19.5 g of iron(III) chloride.

(a) Calculate the number of moles of sodium hydroxide used. [1]
(b) Calculate the number of moles of iron(III) chloride used. [1]
(c) Determine which reactant is the limiting reactant. [1]
(d) Calculate the number of moles of iron(III) hydroxide formed. [1]
(e) Calculate the mass of iron(III) hydroxide formed in g. [1]
(f) Calculate the percentage yield if the mass of iron(III) hydroxide obtained was 7.22 g. Give your answer to 1 decimal place. [2]

Note: The questions in the rest of this chapter will be examined in Unit 2 for Double Award Chemistry

Determining formulae of compounds

28. C_4H_{10} is the formula of butane and C_6H_{14} is the formula of hexane.

(a) Write the empirical formula of butane. [1]
(b) Explain whether C_6H_{14} is a molecular formula or an empirical formula. [1]

1.7 QUANTITATIVE CHEMISTRY

29. The table below gives formulae of some compounds. Complete the table.

Name	Empirical formula	Relative formula mass (M_r)	Molecular formula
ammonia	NH_3	17	
ethene	CH_2	28	
benzene	CH	78	
decane	C_5H_{11}	142	

[4]

30. An oxide with chromium contains 68.4% chromium. Determine the empirical formula of the oxide of chromium. [3]

31. A compound contains 53.3% sulfur and the remainder is iron. Determine the empirical formula of the compound. [3]

32. A chloride of iron contains 34.5% iron. Determine the empirical formula of the chloride of iron. [3]

33. A fluoride of sulfur contains 21.9% sulfur. Determine the empirical formula of the fluoride of sulfur. [3]

34. 13.70 g of an oxide of lead contains 1.28 g of oxygen. Determine the empirical formula of the oxide of lead. [4]

35. An oxide of nitrogen contains 0.14 g of nitrogen and 0.40 g of oxygen. Determine the empirical formula of the oxide of nitrogen. [3]

36. 7.32 g of an oxide of chlorine contains 2.84 g of chlorine. Determine the empirical formula of the compound. [4]

37. A compound contains 3.1 g of phosphorus and 4.8 g of sulfur. Determine the empirical formula of the compound. [3]

38. The following mass measurements were taken during an experiment where a sample of manganese was heated in a crucible.
mass of crucible = 14.22 g
mass of crucible and manganese = 17.52 g
mass of crucible and contents after heating for 5 minutes = 18.55 g
mass of crucible and contents after heating for 10 minutes = 18.80 g
mass of crucible and contents after heating for 15 minutes = 18.80 g

(a) Calculate the mass of manganese used. [1]
(b) Calculate the number of moles of manganese used. [1]
(c) Calculate the mass of oxygen which reacted with the manganese. [1]
(d) Calculate the number of moles of oxygen which reacted with the manganese. [1]
(e) Determine the empirical formula of the oxide of manganese formed. [1]

39. A sample of titanium was heated in air using the apparatus shown below. Mass measurements were taken to determine the formula of the oxide of titanium.

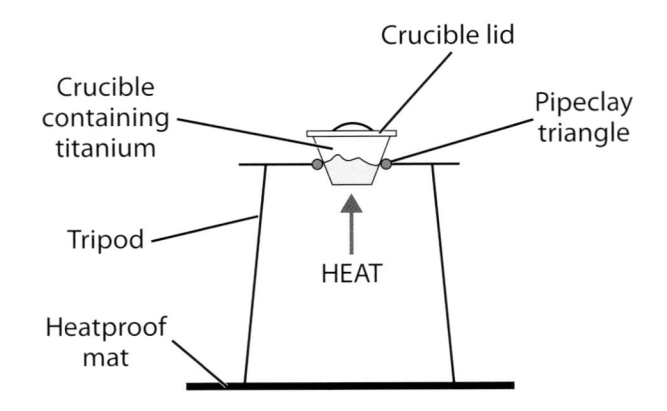

(a) Explain the purpose of the crucible lid. [1]
(b) Explain why it would be important to lift the crucible lid regularly during heating. [1]
(c) How would you ensure that all of the titanium had reacted? [1]
(d) The following mass measurements were taken before and during the reaction.

mass of crucible = 14.25 g
mass of crucible and titanium = 14.97 g
mass of crucible and contents after heating for 3 minutes = 15.25 g
mass of crucible and contents after heating for 6 minutes = 15.40 g
mass of crucible and contents after heating for 9 minutes = 15.45 g
mass of crucible and contents after heating for 12 minutes = 15.45 g

Determine the empirical formula of the oxide of titanium. [5]

40. The table below shows the percentage composition of elements, by mass, in a compound.

Element	Percentage composition (%)
sodium	28.4
chromium	32.1
oxygen	39.5

Determine the empirical formula of the compound. [4]

41. 2.34 g of a compound contains 1.20 g of carbon, 0.22 g of hydrogen, 0.28 g of nitrogen and 0.64 g of oxygen. Determine the empirical formula of the compound. [5]

1.7 QUANTITATIVE CHEMISTRY

42. The following mass measurements were taken when heating a sample of an unknown metal carbonate of formula MCO_3. The metal carbonate decomposes according to the equation:

$$MCO_3 \rightarrow MO + CO_2$$

Mass of crucible = 15.11 g
Mass of crucible and metal carbonate = 18.05 g
Mass of crucible and contents after heating to constant mass = 16.51 g

    (a) Explain how you would ensure you had heated the sample of constant mass. [2]
    (b) Calculate the mass of carbon dioxide released. [1]
    (c) Calculate the number of moles of carbon dioxide released. [1]
    (d) Using the equation given, calculate the number of moles of MCO_3 present in the crucible. [1]
    (e) Using the mass measurements, calculate the mass of MCO_3 present in the crucible initially. [1]
    (f) Using your answers to (d) and (e), calculate the relative formula mass (M_r) of MCO_3. [1]
    (g) Calculate the relative atomic mass of M and identify M. [2]

43. An unknown Group 1 compound, $MClO_3$ decomposes on heating according to the equation:

$$2MClO_3(s) \rightarrow 2MCl(s) + 3O_2(g)$$

19.60 g of $MClO_3$ were heated to constant mass. The mass of the solid remaining was 11.92 g.

    (a) Calculate the mass of oxygen gas released during the reaction. [1]
    (b) Calculate the number of moles of oxygen gas released. [1]
    (c) Using the equation given, calculate the number of moles of $MClO_3$ used in the experiment. [1]
    (d) Using the initial mass and the answer to (c), calculate the relative formula mass (M_r) of $MClO_3$. [1]
    (e) Calculate the relative atomic mass of M and identify M. [2]

Formula involving water of crystallisation

44. 1 mole of hydrated zinc sulfate contains 7 moles of water of crystallisation.
    (a) What is meant by water of crystallisation? [1]
    (b) Write the formula of hydrated zinc sulfate. [1]
    (c) Calculate the relative formula mass of hydrated zinc sulfate. [1]
    (d) Calculate the percentage of water by mass in hydrated zinc sulfate. [2]

45. Hydrated copper(II) chloride, $CuCl_2 \cdot xH_2O$, contains 21.05 % water by mass.
    (a) Calculate the mass of water present in 100 g of the compound. [1]
    (b) Calculate the mass of anhydrous copper(II) chloride present in 100 g of the compound. [1]
    (c) Calculate the number of moles of water present in 100 g of the compound. [1]
    (d) Calculate the number of moles of anhydrous copper(II) chloride present in 100 g of the compound. [1]
    (e) Using your answers to (c) and (d), calculate the degree of hydration and write the formula of hydrated copper(II) chloride. [2]

STRUCTURES, TRENDS, CHEMICAL REACTIONS, QUANTITATIVE CHEMISTRY AND ANALYSIS

46. Hydrated lithium sulfate, $Li_2SO_4 \cdot xH_2O$, contains 14.06 % water by mass. Determine the value of x. [5]

47. Hydrated aluminium nitrate, $Al(NO_3)_3 \cdot xH_2O$ contains 43.2 % water by mass. Determine the value of x. [5]

48. Complete the table below.

Name	Formula	Relative formula mass (M_r)	Percentage of water by mass (%)
hydrated barium chloride	$BaCl_2 \cdot 2H_2O$		
hydrated copper(II) sulfate		250	
hydrated nickel(II) sulfate			44.84
	$Na_2CO_3 \cdot 10H_2O$		

[9]

49. 6.00 g of hydrated chromium(III) nitrate, $Cr(NO_3)_3 \cdot xH_2O$, were heated to constant mass. The mass of anhydrous chromium(III) nitrate remaining was 3.57 g. Determine the value of x. [4]

50. 1.23 g of hydrated magnesium sulfate, $MgSO_4 \cdot xH_2O$, were heated to constant mass. 0.60 g of the anhydrous magnesium sulfate remained.
    (a) What is meant by anhydrous? [1]
    (b) Determine the value of x in $MgSO_4 \cdot xH_2O$. [4]

51. A sample of hydrated sodium carbonate, $Na_2CO_3 \cdot xH_2O$, was heated in a crucible. The following mass measurements were recorded during the experiment.
    mass of crucible = 17.15 g
    mass of crucible and hydrated sodium carbonate = 20.90 g
    mass of crucible and contents after heating to constant mass = 18.74 g

    (a) Explain practically how the sample was heated to constant mass. [2]
    (b) Explain why the sample was heated to constant mass. [1]
    (c) Determine the value of x in $Na_2CO_3 \cdot xH_2O$. [5]

1.7 QUANTITATIVE CHEMISTRY

52. A sample of hydrated iron(II) sulfate, $FeSO_4.xH_2O$, was heated in a crucible. The following mass measurements were recorded during the experiment.
mass of crucible = 16.42 g
mass of crucible and hydrated iron(II) sulfate = 19.20 g
mass of crucible and contents after heating for 5 minutes = 18.24 g
mass of crucible and contents after heating for 10 minutes = 17.94 g
mass of crucible and contents after heating for 15 minutes = 17.94 g

   (a) Explain why the crucible was heated and the mass measured repeatedly during heating. [2]
   (b) Determine the value of x in $FeSO_4.xH_2O$. [5]

53. The equation below shows the reaction which occurs when a sample of hydrated sodium sulfate is heated to constant mass.

$Na_2SO_4.10H_2O \rightarrow Na_2SO_4 + 10H_2O$

   (a) What is meant by the term hydrated? [1]
   (b) Calculate the mass of anhydrous sodium sulfate formed from 1.61 g of hydrated sodium sulfate. [3]
   (c) Calculate the loss in mass observed during the experiment. [1]
   (d) Describe how you would heat a different sample of hydrated sodium sulfate to constant mass including mass measurements taken to allow the degree of hydration to be determined. [4]

1.8 Acids, Bases and Salts

1. Complete the following table giving the colour of the indicator observed with each solution.

Solution	Colour with red litmus	Colour with blue litmus	Colour with universal indicator
hydrochloric acid			
ammonia solution			
sodium hydroxide solution			
water			
ethanoic acid			

[5]

2. Hydrochloric acid is a strong acid. The acid ionisation equation for hydrochloric acid is:

$$HCl \rightarrow H^+ + Cl^-$$

   (a) Name the two ions formed. [2]
   (b) What is meant by a strong acid? [1]
   (c) State another example of a strong acid. [1]
   (d) What colour is observed when methyl orange is added to hydrochloric acid? [1]
   (e) Circle the concentration of hydrochloric acid below which would have the lowest pH.

   0.01 mol/dm³   0.1 mol/dm³   1 mol/dm³

[1]

3. The table below shows the colours with universal indicator for several solutions.

Solution	Colour with universal indicator
A	orange
B	purple
C	yellow
D	blue
E	red

   (a) Which solution would have a pH of 5.8? [1]
   (b) Which solution could be hydrochloric acid? [1]
   (c) Which solution could be a strong alkali? [1]
   (d) Which solution could have a pH of 10? [1]
   (e) What colour would be observed is phenolphthalein was added to solution B? [1]
   (f) Which solution contains the highest concentration of H⁺ ions? [1]

1.8 ACIDS, BASES AND SALTS

4. 10 cm³ of the solutions shown were placed in separate test tubes labelled W, X, Y and Z.

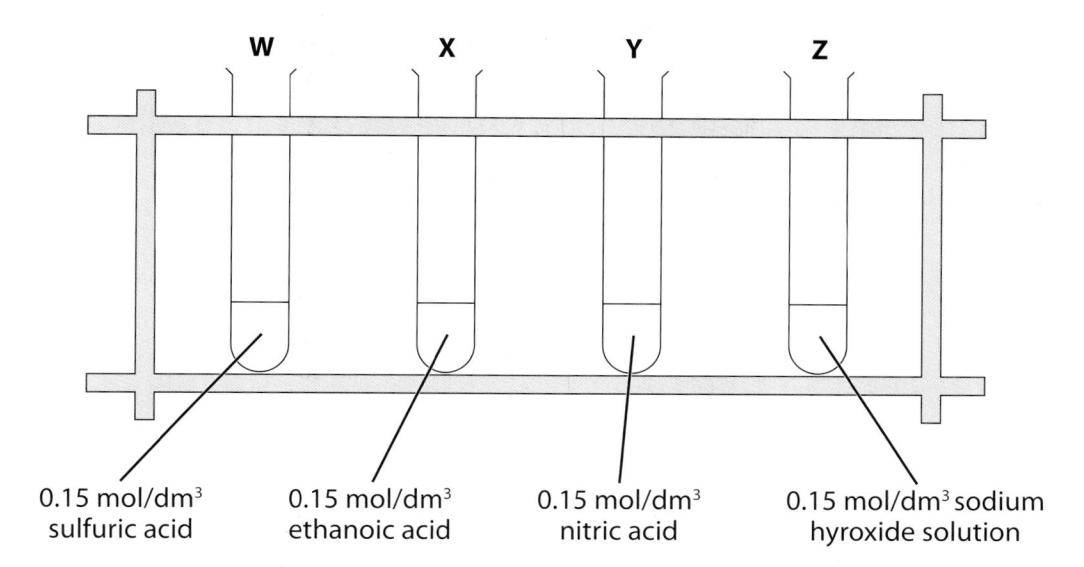

W: 0.15 mol/dm³ sulfuric acid
X: 0.15 mol/dm³ ethanoic acid
Y: 0.15 mol/dm³ nitric acid
Z: 0.15 mol/dm³ sodium hyroxide solution

(a) Describe practically how you would determine the pH of the solutions shown. [2]
(b) Predict which solutions would have the lowest pH and the highest pH. [2]
(c) What colour is observed when methyl orange is added to test tube Z? [1]
(d) Ethanoic acid is a weak acid. What is meant by a weak acid? [1]
(e) Identify the ion in solution Z which causes it to be classified as an alkali? [1]

5. The table below shows five different solutions labelled J, K, L, M and N.
(a) Complete the table giving an approximate pH and colours where required.

Solution	pH	Colour with universal indicator	Colour with methyl orange	Colour with phenolphthalein
J	13			
K		orange		
L	7		orange	
M		red		colourless
N	10			

[5]

(b) Using the letters J, K, L, M and N, answers the questions below.
   (i) Which solution is a strong alkali? [1]
   (ii) Which solution is a weak acid? [1]
   (iii) Which solution is neutral? [1]
   (iv) Which solution(s) would change blue litmus paper to red? [1]

STRUCTURES, TRENDS, CHEMICAL REACTIONS, QUANTITATIVE CHEMISTRY AND ANALYSIS

6. The word equations below show some reactions of acids. Complete the blanks in the equations:
   (a) zinc + hydrochloric acid → _____ + _____ [1]
   (b) _____ + sulfuric acid → sodium sulfate + water [1]
   (c) calcium carbonate + nitric acid → _____ + water + carbon dioxide [1]
   (d) copper(II) oxide + _____ → copper(II) sulfate + _____ [1]
   (e) aluminium hydroxide + hydrochloric acid → _____ + _____ [1]

7. Hydrochloric acid reacts with metals and metal compounds including magnesium metal and copper(II) carbonate. Both reactions produce a gas.
   (a) Using **ONLY** the observations given in the box below, answer the questions which follow.

   | pink solid disappears | grey solid disappears | green solid disappears |
   | colourless solution formed | green solution formed | blue solution formed |

   (i) What two observations may be made when magnesium reacts with hydrochloric acid? [2]
   (ii) What two observations may be made when copper(II) carbonate reacts with hydrochloric acid? [2]

   (b) (i) Write a balanced symbol equation for the reaction of magnesium with hydrochloric acid. [3]
   (ii) Write a balanced symbol equation for the reaction of copper(II) carbonate with hydrochloric acid. [3]

   (c) Describe practically how you would show that the reaction between magnesium and hydrochloric acid is exothermic. [2]

   (d) Complete the table below for the gases produced in the reactions and their tests.

Reaction	Gas produced	Test	Result
magnesium + hydrochloric acid			
copper(II) carbonate + hydrochloric acid			

   [6]

8. Sodium hydroxide solution reacts with hydrochloric acid. The highest temperature achieved was measured during the reaction as 5.0 cm³ portions of hydrochloric acid were added to sodium hydroxide solution in a polystyrene cup with stirring.
   (a) (i) What addition piece of apparatus would be required to add 5.0 cm³ portions of the acid to the polystyrene cup? [1]
   (ii) Explain why a polystyrene cup was used as a container for the reaction. [1]
   (iii) Suggest why the polystyrene cup was placed in a beaker? [1]

(b) The results of the experiment are given in the table below.

Volume of hydrochloric acid added (cm³)	Highest temperature achieved (°C)
0.0	20.0
5.0	24.5
10.0	28.5
15.0	32.0
20.0	35.0
25.0	37.0
30.0	35.5
35.0	34.0
40.0	32.5

(i) Plot the results on the axes below and draw a best fit curve. [4]

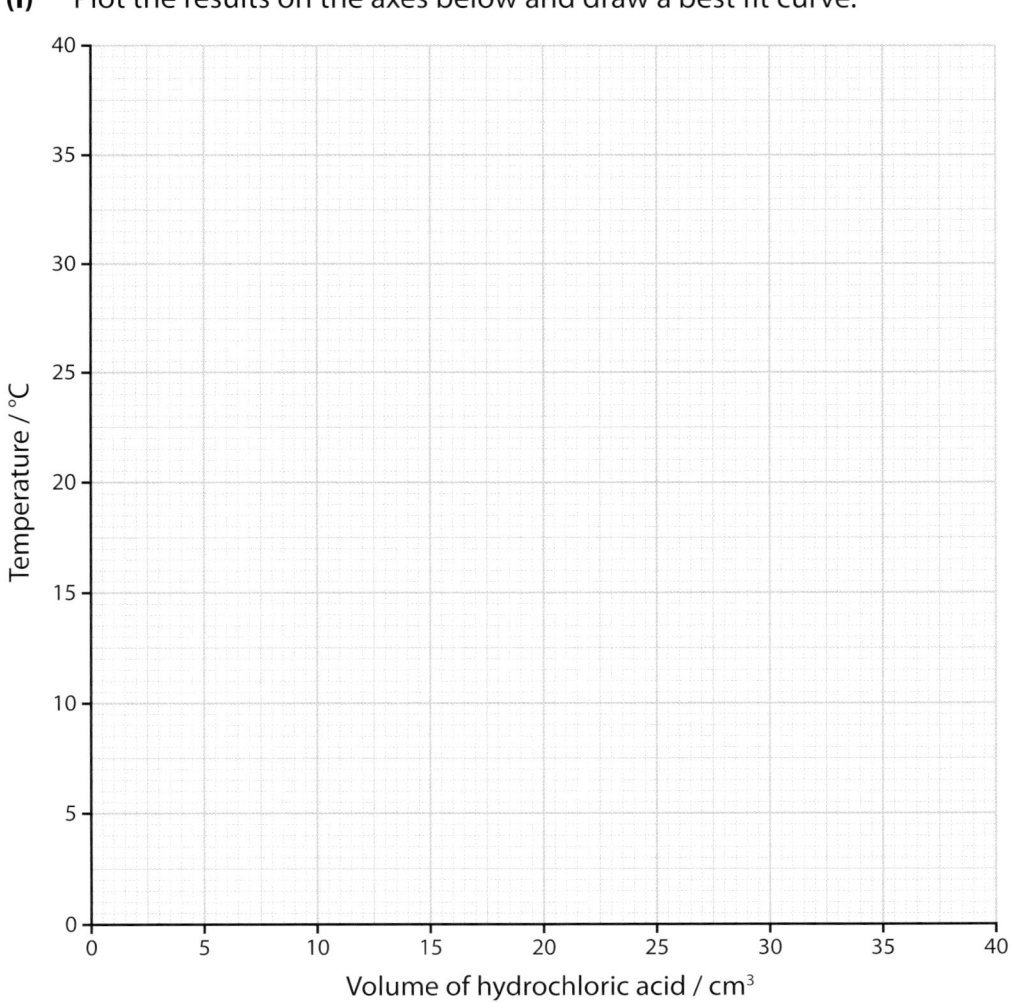

(ii) At what volume of hydrochloric acid is the maximum temperature achieved? [1]
(iii) What was the maximum temperature change? [1]
(iv) Explain whether the reaction is exothermic or endothermic. [1]

(c) The reaction between hydrochloric acid and sodium hydroxide solution is a neutralisation reaction.
    (i) Write a balanced symbol equation for the reaction between hydrochloric acid and sodium hydroxide solution. [2]
    (ii) Write an ionic equation, including state symbols, for the neutralisation reaction. [3]

9. The diagram below shows four different solids which react with sulfuric acid to form a solution of zinc sulfate. Some of the other products are labelled and some are missing and labelled A, B and C.

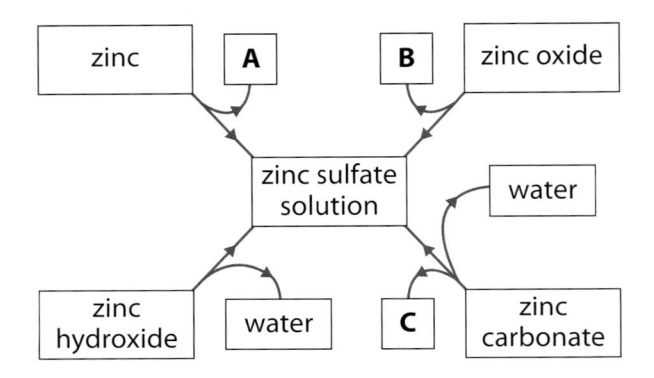

```
   zinc        A          B      zinc oxide
     \         |          |         /
      \        v          v        /
       \                           /
        ----> zinc sulfate <----
              solution  ----> water
       /                           \
      /        ^          ^         \
     /         |          |          \
   zinc      water        C         zinc
 hydroxide                        carbonate
```

(a) Identify A, B and C. [3]
(b) Write a balanced symbol equation for the reaction of zinc hydroxide with sulfuric acid. [3]
(c) (i) Describe how a sample of pure, dry crystals of hydrated zinc sulfate may be obtained using zinc carbonate.
In this question, you will be assessed on the quality of your written communication including the use of specialist scientific terms. [6]
    (ii) Explain why zinc carbonate would be used in preference to zinc oxide in carrying out the preparation of zinc sulfate crystals. [2]
    (iii) Write a balanced symbol equation for the reaction of zinc carbonate with sulfuric acid. [2]

10. The salt potassium sulfate may be prepared from the reaction of potassium hydroxide solution with sulfuric acid.
(a) Write a balanced symbol equation for the reaction of potassium hydroxide with sulfuric acid. [3]
(b) A method for the preparation of a pure, dry sample of the salt is given below.

1. Place 25.0 cm³ of potassium hydroxide solution into a conical flask.
2. Add 3 drops of phenolphthalein indicator.
3. Place the conical flask on a white tile below a burette filled with sulfuric acid.
4. Add sulfuric acid to the flask while swirling the flask until the indicator changes colour.
5. Record the volume of acid used.
6. Repeat using the same volumes without indicator.
7. Heat the solution in an evaporating basin until half volume.
8. Allow to cool and crystallise.
9. Filter off the crystals and dry them.

1.8 ACIDS, BASES AND SALTS

    (i) In step 1, what piece of apparatus could be used to place 25.0 cm³ of potassium hydroxide solution into the conical flask? [1]
    (ii) In step 3, why is flask placed on a white tile? [1]
    (iii) In step 4, what colour change is observed? [2]
    (iv) In step 7, draw a labelled diagram of the assembled apparatus used to heat the solution. [3]
    (v) In step 8, explain why crystals form on cooling. [1]
    (vi) In step 9, state two different methods which could be used to dry the crystals. [2]

11. Salts are formed during reactions of acids.
  (a) What is meant by the term salt? [3]
  (b) Complete the table below.

Acid	Other reactant	Name of salt formed	Formula of the salt	Appearance of the solid salt
nitric acid	sodium carbonate		NaNO₃	white solid
	copper(II) oxide	hydrated copper(II) sulfate	CuSO₄.5H₂O	
hydrochloric acid	potassium hydrogencarbonate			
	ammonia	ammonium nitrate		white solid

[4]
  (c) What colour is solid copper(II) oxide? [1]

  (d) The reaction between solid potassium hydrogencarbonate and hydrochloric acid is endothermic.
    (i) Write a balanced symbol equation for the reaction between potassium hydrogencarbonate and hydrochloric acid. [2]
    (ii) What is observed during this reaction? [3]
    (iii) Describe practically how you would show that the reaction between potassium hydrogencarbonate and hydrochloric acid is endothermic. [2]

  (e) Ammonia reacts with sulfuric acid to form the salt ammonium sulfate.
    (i) Write a balanced symbol equation for the reaction between ammonia and sulfuric acid. [3]
    (ii) The reaction releases heat. What term is used for a reaction which released heat? [1]
    (iii) Some bottles of sulfuric acid have the following hazard symbol on them.

    What does this hazard symbol mean? [1]

1.9 Chemical Analysis

1. The diagrams below show the particles present in different gaseous substances and mixtures. Each differently sized or shaded circle represents a different atom. They are labelled A, B, C, D and E.

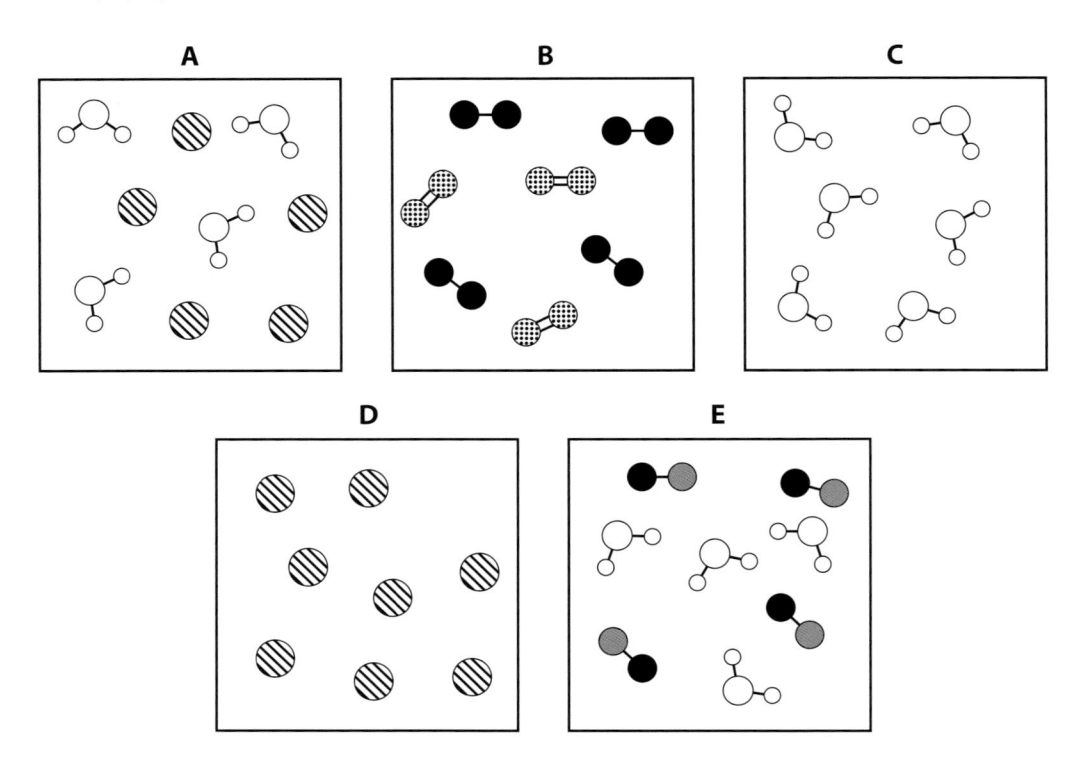

   (a) Which box (A, B, C, D or E) represents a pure element? [1]
   (b) Which box (A, B, C, D or E) represents a pure compound? [1]
   (c) Which box (A, B, C, D or E) represents a mixture of two compounds? [1]
   (d) Which box (A, B, C, D or E) represented a mixture of two elements? [1]

2. A label from a bottle of "pure spring water" is shown below.

PURE SPRING WATER BOTTLED AT SOURCE – CONTENTS (mg/dm³)				
hydrogencarbonate	145	nitrate	2
calcium	41	sodium	7
chloride	5	sulfate	5
magnesium	12		
pH 7.8		Dry residue = 170 mg/dm³	

   (a) Explain why this spring water cannot be described as pure. [1]
   (b) Name and write the formula of one compound present in the spring water. [2]
   (c) They dry residue is the mass of solid remaining on evaporating all the water from a sample of spring water.
      (i) Draw a labelled diagram of the assembled apparatus used to evaporate the water from 25 cm³ of spring water. [3]

(ii) Calculate the mass of residue, in mg, which would be formed on evaporating of all the water from 25 cm³ of a sample of the spring water. [1]

(d) Suggest how the pH of the spring water was measured. [1]
(e) Describe a chemical test for water including the observations for a positive test. [3]

3. A list of separating techniques is given below in the box.

| filtration | distillation | recrystallisation |
| using a separating funnel | evaporation | fractional distillation |

(a) Which technique would be used to obtain water from sea water? [1]
(b) Which technique would be used to obtain salt from salt solution? [1]
(c) Which technique would be used to separate two immiscible liquids? [1]
(d) A diagram of one of the separating techniques is shown below.

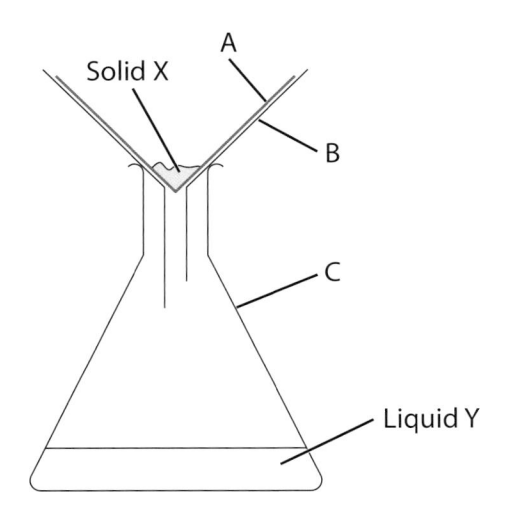

(i) Name this separating technique. [1]
(ii) What labels should be placed at A, B and C? [3]
(iii) State the general name for solid X and liquid Y. [2]
(iv) A mixture of potassium iodide and magnesium oxide was mixed with water. The mixture was stirred well and then separated using the technique shown in (d) above. State the identity of solid X and liquid Y in this experiment. [2]

4. 18 carat "gold" is a formulation which contains 75 % pure gold, 12.5 % silver and 12.5 % copper. It is harder than pure gold so it is often used to make jewellery as it is more durable.
(a) What is meant by the term formulation? [3]
(b) What other term is used for a mixture of elements, at least one of which is a metal? [1]
(c) Give an example of one other formulation. [1]

STRUCTURES, TRENDS, CHEMICAL REACTIONS, QUANTITATIVE CHEMISTRY AND ANALYSIS

(d) The table below shows the melting points of three different carat ratings of gold.

Substance	Melting point (°C)
Pure gold (24 carat)	1063
18 carat "gold"	927
14 carat "gold"	879

   (i) State the relationship between the amount of gold present and the melting point. [1]
   (ii) Circle a value below which could be the melting point for 22 carat "gold".

   860 °C   900 °C   1055 °C   1100 °C

   [1]

5. Water boils at 100 °C. 23.4 g of sodium chloride, NaCl, were dissolved in 100 cm³ of deionised water. The boiling point of the mixture was determined.
   (a) Calculate the number of moles of sodium chloride, NaCl, added. [1]
   (b) Tick the box below which is correct.

   ☐ The boiling point of the mixture is less than 100 °C

   ☐ The boiling point of the mixture is 100 °C

   ☐ The boiling point of the mixture is greater than 100 °C

   [1]

   (c) Complete the passage below using suitable terms.
   Sodium chloride is _____ in water. When sodium chloride dissolves in water, sodium chloride is the _____ and water is the _____.
   The mixture of sodium chloride dissolved in water is called a _____. [4]
   (d) Water in reservoirs goes through several processes before the water is described as potable.
      (i) What is meant by potable water? [1]
      (ii) Describe the processes which water from reservoirs goes through to make it potable. Explain the purpose of each process.
      In this question, you will be assessed on the quality of your written communication including the use of specialist scientific terms. [6]
      (iii) How can sea water be converted into potable water? [1]

1.9 CHEMICAL ANALYSIS

6. The apparatus below shows simple distillation.

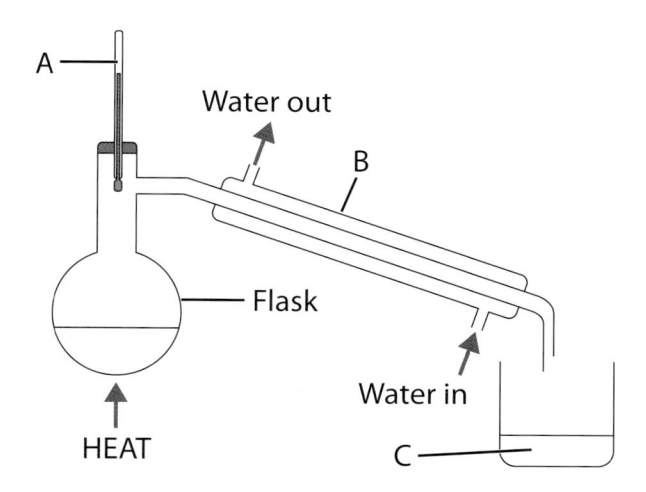

(a) What labels should be placed at A and B? [2]
(b) What general name is given to the liquid collected at C? [1]
(c) Explain how simple distillation separates water from sea water. [2]
(d) What is added to the flask to promote smooth boiling? [1]
(e) How could the apparatus be adapted to achieve a good separation of a mixture of ethanol (boiling point 79 °C) and water? [1]

7. A paper chromatogram experiment was carried out on a black dye. The solvent used was dilute hydrochloric acid. The dye separated into three components labelled X, Y and Z on the chromatogram shown below.

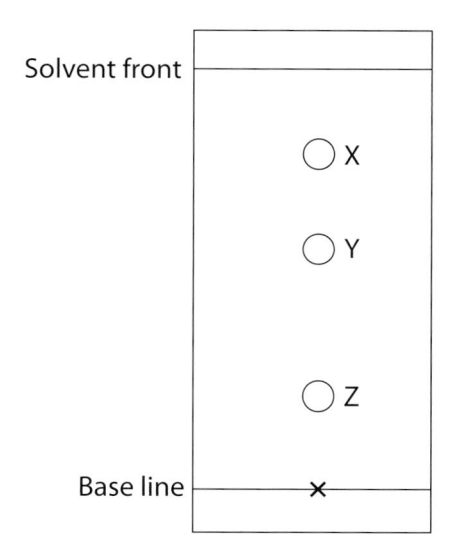

(a) Describe how the paper chromatography experiment was carried out to achieve the results shown above. [4]
(b) Explain why the base line is drawn in pencil. [1]

STRUCTURES, TRENDS, CHEMICAL REACTIONS, QUANTITATIVE CHEMISTRY AND ANALYSIS

(c) Calculate the R_f value for component labelled Z. Give your answer to 2 decimal places. **Show your working out**.

$R_f =$ _____ [3]

(d) Which spot is most soluble in the solvent? [1]

(e) Explain, with reference to the mobile phase and the stationary phase, how the process of paper chromatography separates the components in a dye. [3]

8. The following tests were carried out on a solid sample of an ionic compound, labelled A.

Test	Observations
1. Make a solution of the solid A in approximately 15 – 20 cm³ of deionised water. Divide the solution into three test tubes. Carry out tests 2, 3 and 4 using the solution in these test tubes.	Solid A dissolves to form a blue solution.
2. Add 5 drops of silver nitrate solution to the solution of A in the first test tube.	White precipitate.
3. Add 5 drops of sodium hydroxide solution to the solution of A in the second test tube followed by excess sodium hydroxide solution.	Blue precipitate which remains on addition of excess sodium hydroxide solution.
4. Add 5 drops of ammonia solution to the solution of A in the third test tube followed by excess ammonia solution.	Blue precipitate which is soluble in excess ammonia solution forming a deep blue solution.
5. Carry out a flame test on the solid.	Blue–green flame.

(a) Identify the white precipitate formed in test 2. [1]
(b) Write an ionic equation, including state symbols, for the formation of the blue precipitate in test 3. [4]
(c) Explain how a flame test is carried out on solid A. [3]
(d) Identify the cation and anion present in A. [2]
(e) Write the formula for compound A. [1]

1.9 CHEMICAL ANALYSIS

9. Some qualitative tests were carried out on different ionic compounds.
   (a) Identify the ions present based on the results of the tests.
   - **(i)** A white precipitate was formed when barium chloride solution was added to a solution of a compound. [1]
   - **(ii)** A green precipitate was formed when sodium hydroxide solution was added to a solution of a compound. The precipitate remained when excess sodium hydroxide solution was added. [1]
   - **(iii)** A yellow precipitate was formed when silver nitrate solution was added to a solution of a compound. [1]
   - **(iv)** A colourless gas was produced when dilute nitric acid was added to a solid compound. The gas changed limewater from colourless to milky. [1]
   - **(v)** A lilac flame was observed when a flame test was carried out on a solid sample of a compound. [1]
   - **(vi)** A white precipitate was formed when ammonia solution was added to a solution of a compound. The precipitate remained in excess ammonia solution. A white precipitate was also formed when sodium hydroxide solution was added to a fresh sample of a solution of the same compound. The precipitate was soluble in excess sodium hydroxide solution. [1]

   (b) (i) Write an ionic equation for the formation of the white precipitate in (a)(i). [2]
   - **(ii)** Identify the green precipitate formed in (a)(ii). [1]
   - **(iii)** Identify the yellow precipitate formed in (a)(iii). [1]
   - **(iv)** Identify the colourless gas produced in (a)(iv). [1]
   - **(v)** Write an ionic equation for the formation of the white precipitate in (a)(vi) when sodium hydroxide solution was added. [3]

1.10 Solubility

1. In determining the solubility of a solid in water, the following procedure was used.

   4.0 g of potassium chlorate were placed in 10.0 g of water in a boiling tube at 20 °C. The mixture was heated in a water bath, while stirring with a thermometer, until all of the solid dissolved.
   The solution was allowed to cool, with continuous stirring, until crystals started to form and the temperature was recorded (temperature = 81 °C).
   The solution was heated again until the solid dissolved and again allowed the cool and the temperature at which crystals started to form was recorded (temperature = 79 °C).

   (a) Calculate the average temperature at which crystals started to form. [1]
   (b) Suggest why the experiment was repeated. [1]
   (c) Calculate the solubility in g/100 g water at 80 °C. [1]
   (d) State one possible source of error in this experiment and one way in which you could minimise this source of error. [2]

2. (a) What is meant by the term solubility? [3]
   (b) Some solubility data for aluminium sulfate is given in the table below.

Temperature (°C)	0	20	40	60	80	100
Solubility (g/100 g water)	31	36	46	59	73	89

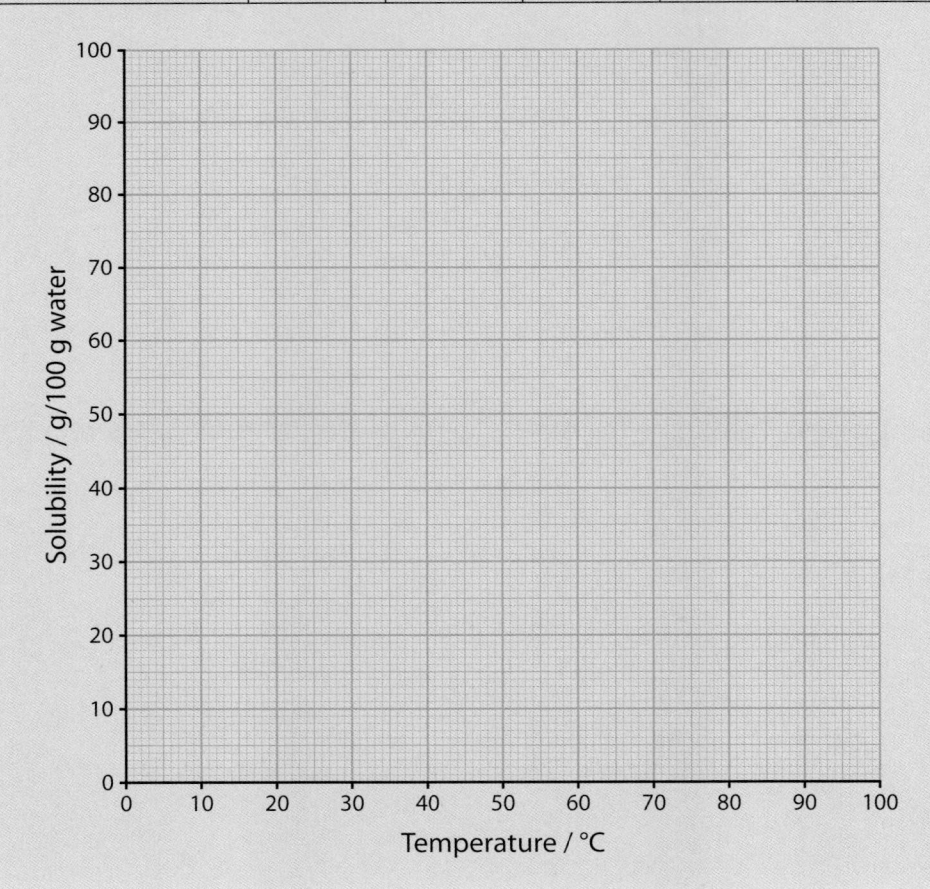

1.10 SOLUBILITY

(i) Plot the solubility curve for aluminium sulfate on the axes on the previous page. [4]
(ii) Using your graph, determine the solubility of aluminium sulfate in g/100 g water at 70 °C. [1]
(iii) A solution containing 150 g of aluminium sulfate in 250 g of water at 80 °C was cooled and 60 g of solid aluminium sulfate were deposited. Calculate the temperature to which the solution was cooled. [3]
(iv) A saturated solution of aluminium sulfate containing 40 g of water at 50 °C was cooled to 25 °C. Calculate the mass of solid deposited. [4]

3. The graph below shows the solubility curves for potassium chlorate and potassium nitrate.

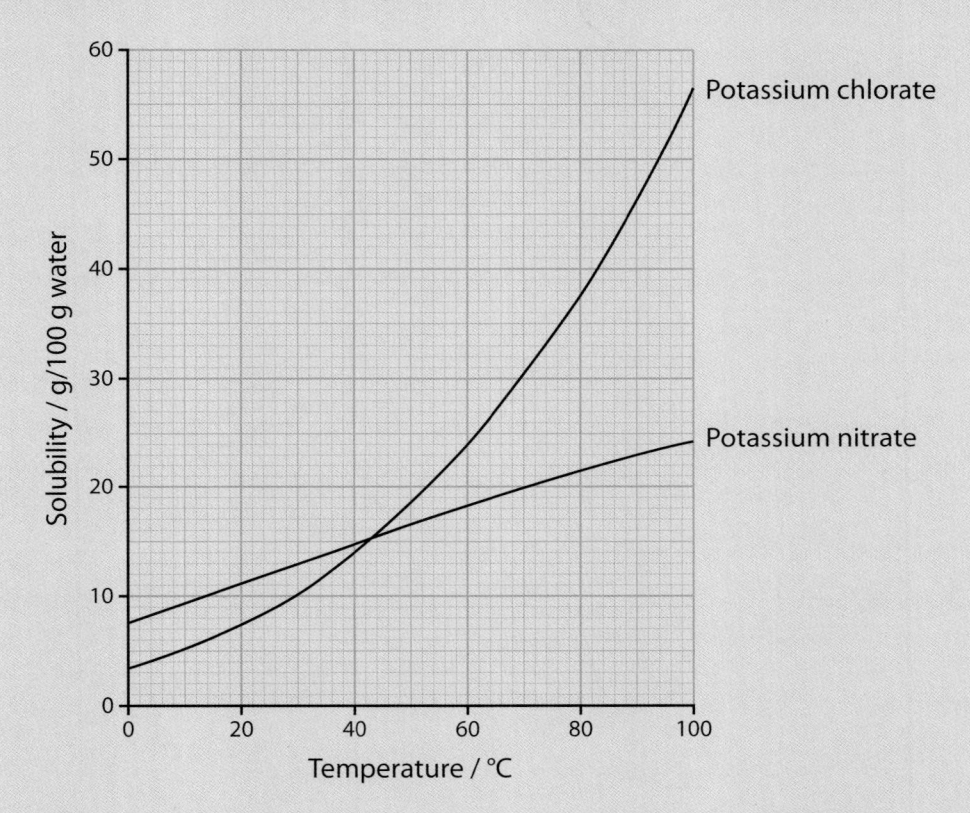

(a) At what temperature is the solubility of the two compounds the same? [1]
(b) State the trend in solubility for potassium nitrate. [1]
(c) Using the graph, determine the mass of potassium nitrate, in grams, required to saturate 80 g of water at 20 °C. [2]
(d) Using the graph determine the mass of potassium chlorate, in grams, which would crystallise when a saturated solution containing 25 g of water at 90 °C is cooled to 40 °C. [3]

(e) (i) Using the graphs, complete the table below by determining the solubility at the given temperatures. [3]

Solid	Temperature (°C)	Solubility at given temperature (g/100 g water)
potassium chlorate	60	
potassium nitrate	60	
potassium chlorate	70	

(ii) Three different mixtures, A, B and C were prepared as detailed below. Using the information in the table above, state and explain which of the mixtures below would be saturated and which would be unsaturated. [3]

Mixture	Solid	Mass of solid (g)	Mass of water (g)	Temperature (°C)
A	potassium chlorate	20	100	60
B	potassium nitrate	20	100	60
C	potassium chlorate	4	10	70

4. The table below gives the solubility values of hydrogen chloride gas and solid potassium chloride in water at different temperatures.

Temperature (°C)	0	20	40	60	80	100
Solubility of hydrogen chloride (g/100 g water)	81	70	61	53	47	40
Solubility of potassium chloride (g/100 g water)	28	34	40	46	51	56

(a) What name is given to a solution of hydrogen chloride gas in water? [1]

(b) State the trend in the solubility of hydrogen chloride gas with increasing temperature. [1]

(c) The graph below shows the solubility curve for potassium chloride.

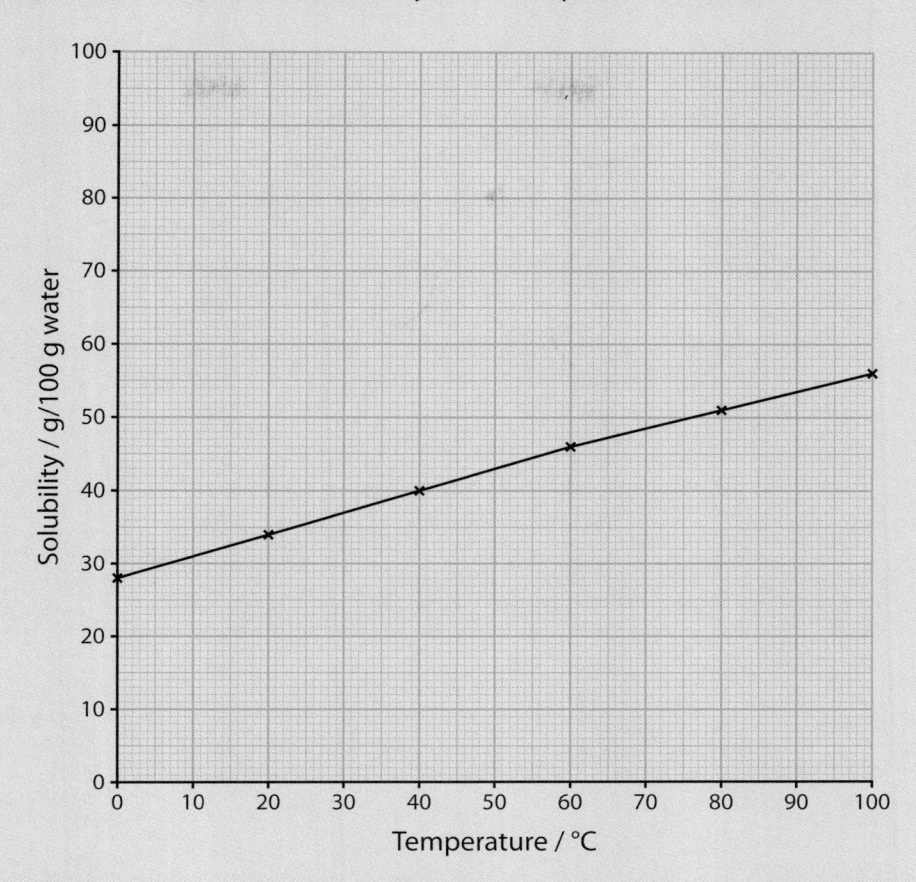

(i) On the same axes, plot the solubility curve for hydrogen chloride gas. [4]
(ii) At what temperature do potassium chloride and hydrogen chloride gas have the same solubility? [1]
(iii) Calculate the minimum mass of water required to dissolve 148 g of potassium chloride at 30 °C. [3]
(iv) Calculate the mass of hydrogen chloride which would saturate 60 g of water at 20 °C. [2]
(v) A saturated solution of potassium chloride at 50 °C containing 50 g of water was cooled to a lower temperature and 6 g of solid was deposited. Calculate the temperature to which the solution was cooled. [3]

Unit 2
Further Chemical Reactions, Rates and Equilibrium, Calculations and Organic Chemistry

2.1 Metals and Reactivity Series

1. Metals vary in their reactivity with air, water and steam.

   (a) Using the metals listed in the box below, answer the questions which follow.

aluminium	calcium	copper	iron
magnesium	potassium	sodium	zinc

   (i) Which metal burns in air with a brick red flame forming a white solid? [1]
   (ii) Which metal glows on heating in air and the surface becomes black? [1]
   (iii) Which metal forms a yellow solid on heating but changes to a white solid on cooling? [1]
   (iv) Which metal sinks and then floats in water? [1]
   (v) Which metal floats on water and burns on the surface with a lilac flame? [1]

   (b) Write balanced symbol equations for the following reactions.
   (i) magnesium burning in air. [3]
   (ii) sodium reacting with water. [3]
   (iii) zinc reacting with steam. [2]
   (iv) potassium burning in air. [3]

2. Magnesium reacts with steam when heated. The apparatus below is used to heat magnesium in steam.

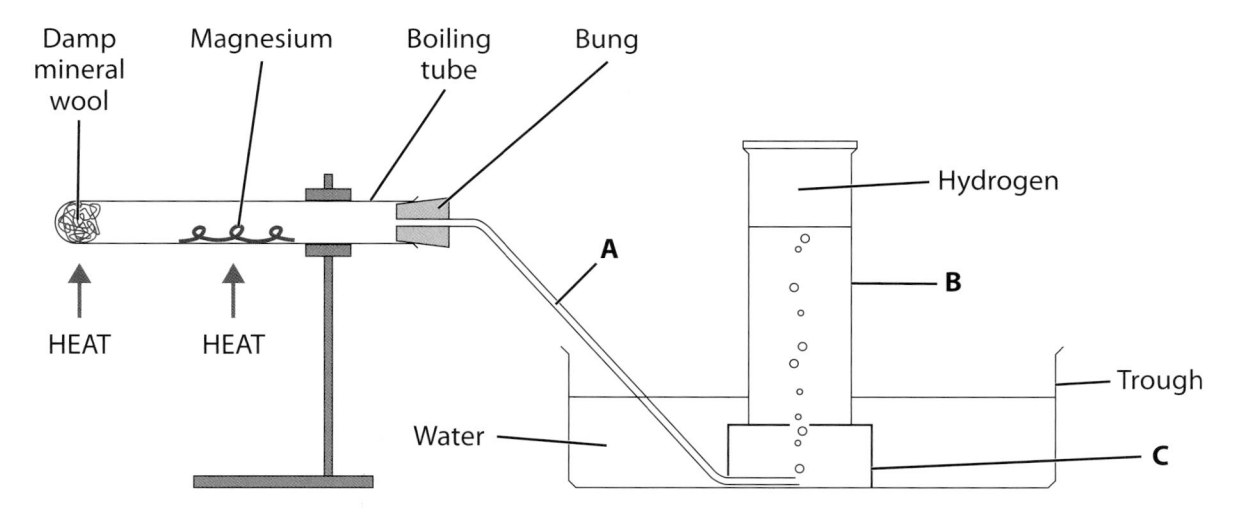

   (a) What labels should be placed at **A**, **B** and **C**? [3]
   (b) Explain why the damp mineral wool is heated. [1]
   (c) What is observed during the reaction? [2]
   (d) Write a balanced symbol equation for the reaction of magnesium with steam. Include state symbols. [3]
   (e) Why should the bung be removed from the boiling tube when heating stops? [1]

FURTHER CHEMICAL REACTIONS, RATES AND EQUILIBRIUM, CALCULATIONS AND ORGANIC CHEMISTRY

3. A series of displacement reactions was carried out with 6 metals and solutions of the metal nitrates. The results are shown in the table below. A tick (✓) indicates that a reaction occurs.

Metal	zinc nitrate	iron(II) nitrate	copper(II) nitrate	tin(II) nitrate	aluminium nitrate	cobalt(II) nitrate
zinc		✓	✓	✓	✗	✓
iron	✗		✓	✓	✗	✓
copper	✗	✗		✗	✗	✗
tin	✗	✗	✓		✗	✗
aluminium	✓	✓	✓	✓		✓
cobalt	✗	✗	✓	✓	✗	

A reactivity series is given below from most reactive to least reactive.

aluminium

zinc

iron

copper

(a) Using the information in the table place tin and cobalt in the reactivity series above. [2]
(b) Explain why a reaction occurs between zinc and copper(II) nitrate. [2]
(c) Write a balanced symbol equation for the reaction between aluminium and copper(II) nitrate solution. [3]
(d) The balanced symbol equation for the reaction between zinc and iron(II) nitrate is:

$$Zn(s) + Fe(NO_3)_2(aq) \rightarrow Zn(NO_3)_2(aq) + Fe(s)$$

(i) Write an ionic equation for this reaction. [2]
(ii) Complete the half equation below for the reaction of zinc.

$$Zn \rightarrow \underline{\hspace{2cm}} + \underline{\hspace{1cm}} e^-$$

[2]

(iii) Complete the half equation below for the reaction of iron(II) ions.

$$Fe^{2+} + \underline{\hspace{2cm}} \rightarrow \underline{\hspace{2cm}}$$

[2]

2.1 METALS AND REACTIVITY SERIES

4. (a) Calcium metal reacts with water. The reaction releases heat and bubbles of gas are observed.

   (i) Write a balanced symbol equation for the reaction of calcium with water. [3]

   (ii) State two other observations which occur during this reaction. [2]

   (iii) The diagram below shows the reaction of calcium and water in a beaker. Complete the three missing labels on the diagram. [3]

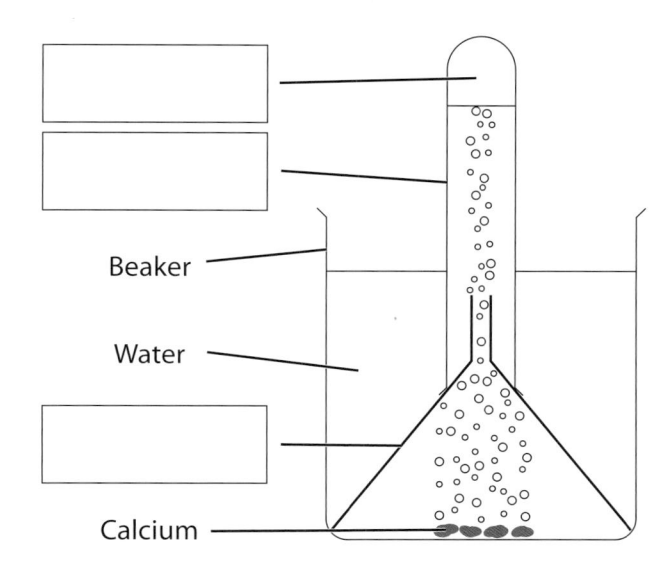

(Diagram labels shown: Beaker, Water, Calcium)

(b) Potassium also reacts with water releasing heat and fizzing on the surface of the water as a gas is produced.

   (i) Write a balanced symbol equation for the reaction of potassium with water. Include state symbols. [4]

   (ii) State three other observations which occur when potassium reacts with water. [3]

5. Explain the processes involved in extracting copper metal from soil by phytomining.

In this question, you will be assessed on the quality of your written communication including the use of specialist scientific terms.

[6]

6. Metals vary in their reactivity and method of extraction from the Earth.

   (a) Explain, in terms of electrons, why potassium is more reactive than sodium. [2]

   (b) Write a half equation for the formation of a calcium ion from a calcium atom. [3]

   (c) Explain why aluminium is extracted from its ore by electrolysis whereas iron is extracted by chemical reduction using carbon monoxide. [2]

2.2 Redox, Rusting and Iron

1. Rust is formed when iron reacts with an element and a compound.

   (a) Name the element and the compound which react with iron to form rust. [2]
   (b) What is the chemical name for rust? [2]
   (c) Describe the appearance of rust. [2]
   (d) Explain why rusting is described as an oxidation reaction. [2]

2. Equations for different reactions are shown in the table below.

Reaction	Equation
A	$H_2 + Br_2 \rightarrow 2HBr$
B	$Fe_2O_3 + 3CO \rightarrow 2Fe + 3CO_2$
C	$2Al + Fe_2O_3 \rightarrow 2Fe + Al_2O_3$
D	$Cl_2 + 2e^- \rightarrow 2Cl^-$
E	$2Ca + O_2 \rightarrow 2CaO$

   (a) Explain why bromine is described as being reduced in reaction A. [2]
   (b) What is oxidised in reaction B? [1]
   (c) What is reduced in reaction C? [1]
   (d) Explain, in terms of electrons, why reaction D is described as a reduction reaction. [2]
   (e) Explain, in terms of electrons, why calcium is described as being oxidised in reaction E. [2]

3. Hydrogen sulfide reacts with oxygen according to the word equation:

   hydrogen sulfide + oxygen → sulfur dioxide + water

   (a) Write a balanced symbol equation for this reaction. [3]
   (b) What element is oxidised in this reaction? [1]
   (c) Explain your answer to (b). [2]
   (d) Sulfur dioxide reacts with fluorine and water as shown below:

   $$SO_2 + F_2 + 2H_2O \rightarrow 2HF + H_2SO_4$$

   Explain why fluorine is described as being reduced in this reaction. [2]

2.2 REDOX, RUSTING AND IRON

4. The experiment below was set up to investigate rusting. Rust formed on the surface of the iron nail in test tube 1.

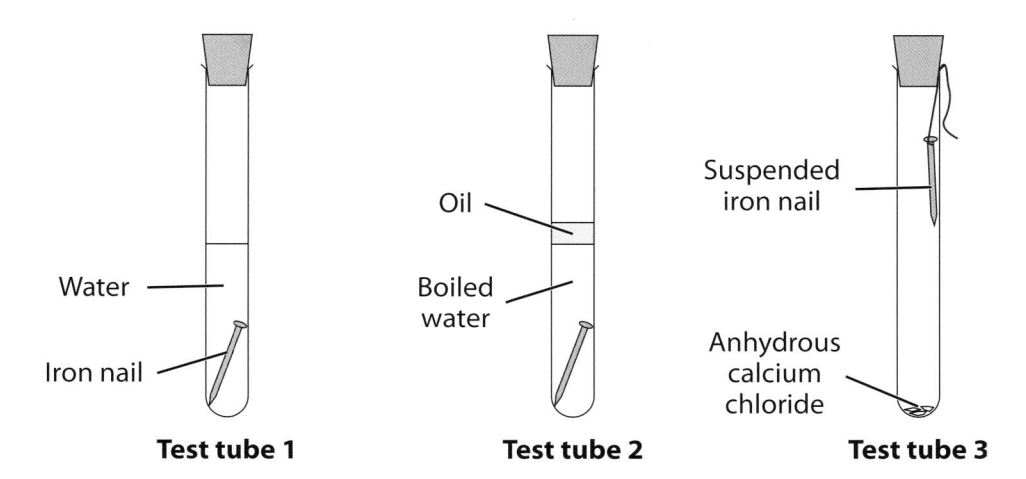

Test tube 1: Water, Iron nail
Test tube 2: Oil, Boiled water
Test tube 3: Suspended iron nail, Anhydrous calcium chloride

(a) Explain why no rust formed on the iron nail in test tube 2. [2]
(b) Explain why no rust formed on the iron nail in test tube 3. [2]
(c) What conditions are required for rust to form? [2]

5. An iron bucket may be coated in zinc metal. The zinc acts as a barrier to prevent the formation of rust. However if the zinc coating is scratched, the zinc also prevents the iron from rusting by sacrificial protection.

(a) State two other barrier methods of preventing iron from rusting. [2]
(b) Explain how zinc prevents rusting by sacrificial protection. [2]
(c) Name one other metal which may be used for sacrificial protection. [1]
(d) What name is given to coating iron in zinc? [1]

6. Iron is extracted from its ore in the Blast Furnace. Materials added to the blast furnace contain a chemical which is required for the production of iron.

(a) Complete the table, giving the name of the material added to the Blast Furnace which contains the chemicals shown.

Main chemical component required in Blast Furnace	Material added
iron(III) oxide	
calcium carbonate	
carbon	
oxygen	

[4]

(b) Explain, using balanced symbol equations, how carbon and oxygen react in two steps to form carbon monoxide in the Blast Furnace. [5]
(c) What is the role of carbon monoxide in the Blast Furnace? [1]

FURTHER CHEMICAL REACTIONS, RATES AND EQUILIBRIUM, CALCULATIONS AND ORGANIC CHEMISTRY

  (d) Write a balanced symbol equation for the production of iron from iron(III) oxide in the Blast Furnace. [3]
  (e) Calcium carbonate helps to remove acidic impurities in the Blast Furnace. The word equations below show the reactions involved.

  Reaction 1: calcium carbonate → calcium oxide + carbon dioxide

  Reaction 2: calcium oxide + silicon dioxide → calcium silicate

   (i) What type of reaction is occurring in reaction 1? [1]
   (ii) Write a balanced symbol equation for reaction 1. [2]
   (iii) From the chemicals in the reactions above, name the acidic impurity. [1]
   (iv) What is the common name for calcium silicate? [1]
   (v) Write a balanced symbol equation for reaction 2. [2]
   (vi) Explain how the calcium silicate is removed from the Blast Furnace. [1]

7. Magnesium reacts with copper(II) sulfate solution according to the equation below:

   $$Mg(s) + CuSO_4(aq) \rightarrow MgSO_4(aq) + Cu(s)$$

   (a) What colour change in the solution would be observed when excess magnesium is added to copper(II) sulfate solution? [2]
   (b) Explain, in terms of reactivity, why magnesium reacts with copper(II) sulfate solution. [2]
   (c) Explain, in terms of electrons, why this reaction is described as a redox reaction.
   In this question, you will be assessed on the quality of your written communication including the use of specialist scientific terms. [6]
   (d) Name one other metal which would react safely with copper(II) sulfate solution. [1]

8. Zinc reacts with iron(II) nitrate solution producing zinc nitrate and iron. The reaction is a redox reaction and it is exothermic. The green solution of iron(II) nitrate fades to colourless.

   (a) Write a balanced symbol equation for this reaction. [2]
   (b) State one other term used to describe this type of reaction. [1]
   (c) Write an ionic equation for this reaction. [2]
   (d) Zinc is oxidised during this reaction.
      (i) Write a half equation for the oxidation reaction occurring. [3]
      (ii) Explain why zinc is described as being oxidised. [2]
   (e) Iron(II) ions are reduced during this reaction.
      (i) Write a half equation for the reduction reaction occurring. [3]
      (ii) Explain why iron(II) ions are described as being reduced. [2]
   (f) What is meant by the terms redox and exothermic? [2]

2.3 Rates of Reaction

1. Three different catalysts were used in the decomposition of hydrogen peroxide. The table below shows the time taken for all of the hydrogen peroxide to decompose using the different catalysts.

Catalyst	Time (s)
copper(II) oxide	150
lead(II) oxide	345
zinc oxide	820

   (a) State which catalyst from the table above is the least effective and explain your answer. [2]
   (b) What is meant by the term catalyst? [2]
   (c) A catalyst provides an alternative reaction pathway of lower activation energy. What is meant by the term activation energy? [1]

2. Zinc reacts with hydrochloric acid according to the equation below:

   $$Zn(s) + 2HCl(aq) \rightarrow ZnCl_2(aq) + H_2(g)$$

   In an experiment, 0.01 moles of hydrochloric were placed in a conical flask and 0.39 g of zinc were added.

   (a) What piece of apparatus could be used to measure the volume of gas produced in this reaction? [1]
   (b) (i) Calculate the number of moles of zinc used. [1]
       (ii) Which reactant is the limiting reactant? [1]
       (iii) Calculate the number of moles of hydrogen gas which could be formed in this experiment. [1]
       (iv) Calculate the volume of hydrogen gas, in cm³, which could be formed in this experiment. [1]
   (c) Suggest why the total volume of gas measured in this experiment may be less than the volume you calculated in **(b)(iv)** above. [1]

3. Calcium carbonate reacts with nitric acid. The reaction produces a gas and mass is lost. The mass can be monitored to measure the rate of the reaction.

   (a) Write a balanced symbol equation for the reaction of calcium carbonate with nitric acid. [3]
   (b) 2.0 g of calcium carbonate were reacted with an excess of hydrochloric acid at 20 °C. The reaction was carried out in a conical flask with a cotton wool plug in the neck of the flask. The flask was placed on an electronic balance and mass measurements were taken every 20 seconds.
       (i) Draw a labelled diagram of the assembled apparatus used to carry out this experiment. [4]

FURTHER CHEMICAL REACTIONS, RATES AND EQUILIBRIUM, CALCULATIONS AND ORGANIC CHEMISTRY

The graph below shows the results of the experiment.

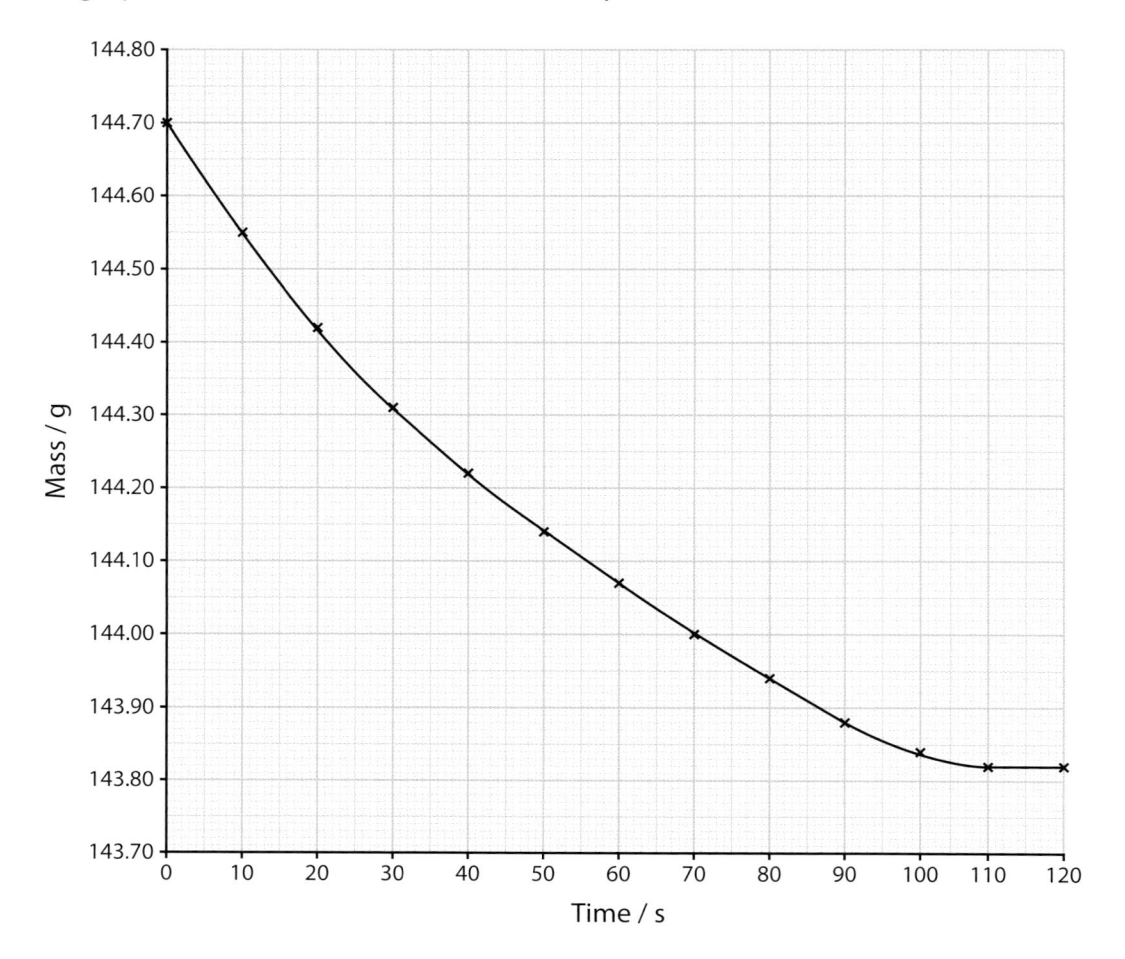

(ii) What was the total loss in mass during the reaction? [1]
(iii) At what time was the mass 144.00 g? [1]
(iv) The experiment was repeated at 40 °C with all other factors being kept the same. Sketch the curve you would expected to obtain and label it A. [1]
(v) Calculate the theoretical loss in mass if 0.5 g of calcium carbonate were used with excess hydrochloric acid. [3]

(c) State and explain the effect of using the same mass of larger solid pieces of calcium carbonate on the rate of the reaction. [3]

4. Sodium thiosulfate, $Na_2S_2O_3$, reacts with hydrochloric acid to form sodium chloride, sulfur, sulfur dioxide and water. As the solid sulfur is formed, the solution becomes cloudy.

(a) Write a balanced symbol equation for the reaction of sodium thiosulfate with hydrochloric acid. [3]
(b) 25.0 cm³ of sodium thiosulfate solution were mixed with 25.0 cm³ of hydrochloric acid in a conical flask sitting on a cross marked on white paper. The time taken for the cross to no longer be visible when viewed from above was measured.

2.3 RATES OF REACTION

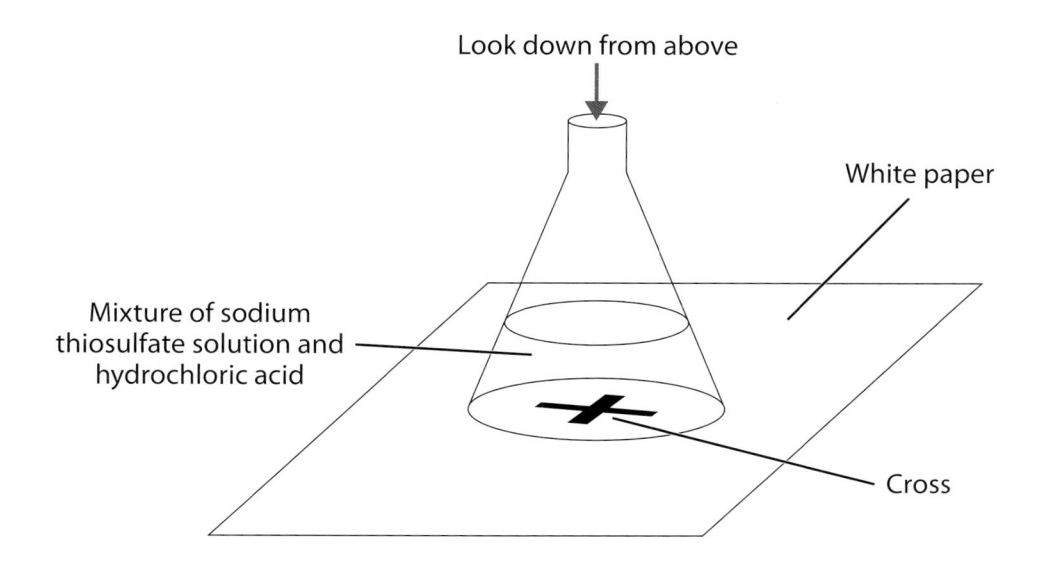

Look down from above ↓

White paper

Mixture of sodium thiosulfate solution and hydrochloric acid

Cross

The table below gives some of the results of the experiments.

Experiment	Concentration of sodium thiosulfate solution (mol/dm³)	Concentration of hydrochloric acid (mol/dm³)	Time (s)	Rate (s⁻¹)
1	0.8	0.2		
2	0.4	0.2	40	0.025
3	0.4	0.1	80	0.0125
4	0.2	0.1	160	0.00625
5		0.1	320	0.003125

(i) How is the rate in the table above calculated? [1]
(ii) Predict the values for the time and rate for the experiment 1 based on the other results. Put these results in the table. [2]
(iii) Explain, in terms of particles, how decreasing the concentration of hydrochloric acid affects the rate of reaction. [4]
(iv) What concentration of sodium thiosulfate would give the rate of reaction listed in experiment 5? [1]

5. Magnesium ribbon reacts with hydrochloric acid. The reaction produces a gas. The equation for the reaction is:

$$Mg(s) + 2HCl(aq) \rightarrow MgCl_2(aq) + H_2(g)$$

0.1 g of magnesium ribbon were reacted with 25.0 cm³ of 0.25 mol/dm³ hydrochloric acid at 20 °C in a conical flask. The volume of gas produced was recorded every 10 seconds using a gas syringe. The magnesium ribbon is in excess.

(a) Draw a labelled diagram of the assembled apparatus used to carry out this experiment. [4]

(b) The graph below shows the results of the experiment.

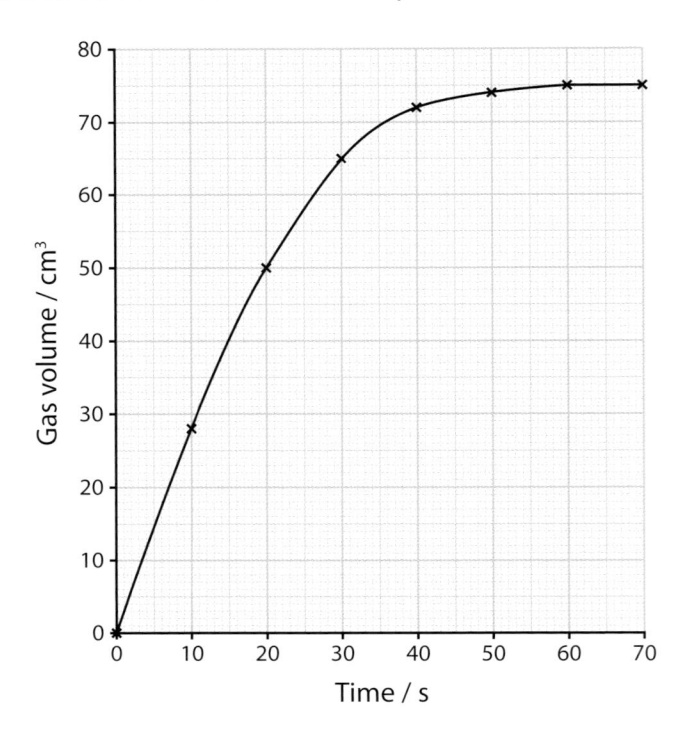

(i) At what time did the reaction finish? [1]

(ii) During which time period below was the reaction fastest?
Circle the correct answer.

0 – 10 s   10 – 20 s   20 – 30 s   30 – 40 s   40 – 50 s   50 – 60 s   [1]

(iii) What was the total volume of gas produced in the experiment? [1]

(iv) Sketch the graph you would expect to obtain if the experiment were repeated using 0.1 g of magnesium ribbon with 25.0 cm³ of 0.25 mol/dm³ hydrochloric acid at 50 °C. Label this graph A. [1]

(v) Sketch the graph you would expect to obtain if the experiment were repeated using 0.1 g of magnesium ribbon with 25.0 cm³ of 0.20 mol/dm³ hydrochloric acid at 20 °C. Label this graph B. [2]

2.3 RATES OF REACTION

6. Hydrogen peroxide solution decomposes in the presence of a catalyst to produce oxygen gas as one of the products.

(a) Write a balanced symbol equation for the decomposition of hydrogen peroxide solution. Include state symbols. [4]

(b) Name the catalyst which is used when carrying out this reaction in the laboratory. [1]

(c) What is meant by the term catalyst? [2]

(d) Explain how a catalyst causes a change in the rate of reaction. [2]

(e) 25.0 cm³ of 1.2 mol/dm³ hydrogen peroxide solution were placed in a conical flask. The conical flask was placed on an electronic balance. 1.0 g of a solid catalyst was added and the mass recorded every 10 seconds. The reaction was carried out at 20 °C. The results are shown on the following graph.

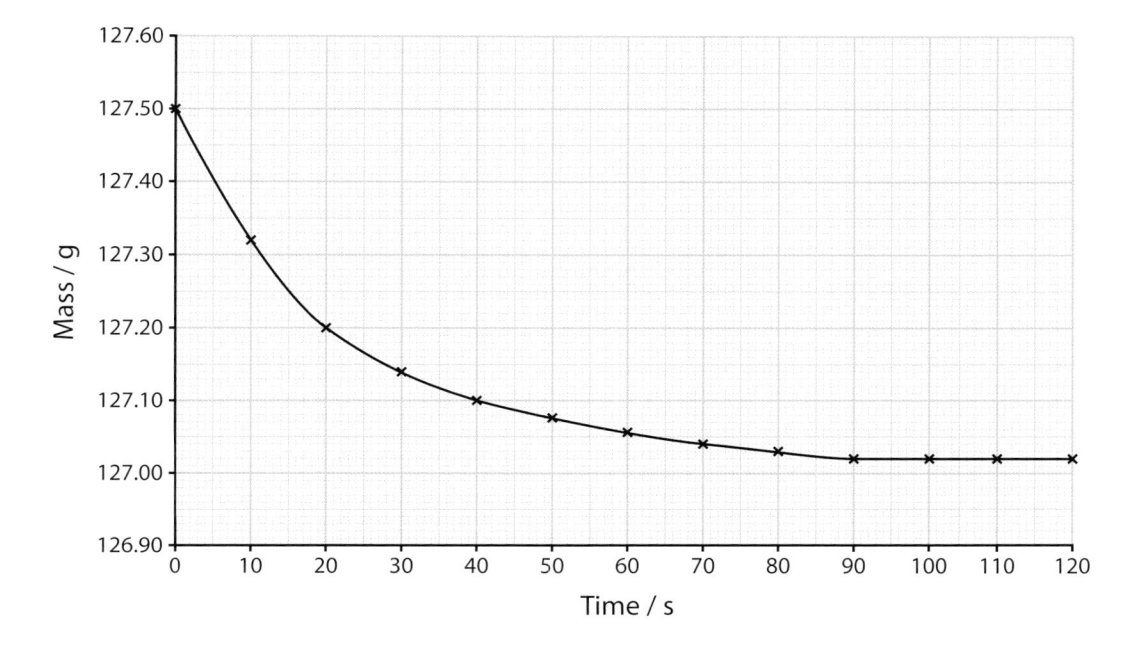

(i) At what time did the reaction finish? [1]

(ii) What was the total loss in mass during the reaction? [1]

(iii) The experiment was repeated using 25.0 cm³ of 1.2 mol/dm³ hydrogen peroxide solution and 1.0 g of the same solid catalyst at 40 °C. Sketch a graph of the results you would expect to obtain under these conditions and label it A. [1]

(iv) The experiment was repeated at 20 °C using 25.0 cm³ of 1.0 mol/dm³ hydrogen peroxide solution. Predict the loss in mass which would occur. [1]

(v) Sketch the graph you would expect to obtain under the conditions given in (iv) above. Label this graph B. [1]

(vi) Predict what mass of catalyst you would expect to remain at the end of the experiment and explain your answer. [2]

FURTHER CHEMICAL REACTIONS, RATES AND EQUILIBRIUM, CALCULATIONS AND ORGANIC CHEMISTRY

7. Magnesium reacts with hydrochloric acid. The points plotted on the graph below show the values obtained for the rate of reaction for different concentrations of hydrochloric acid reacting with excess magnesium ribbon.

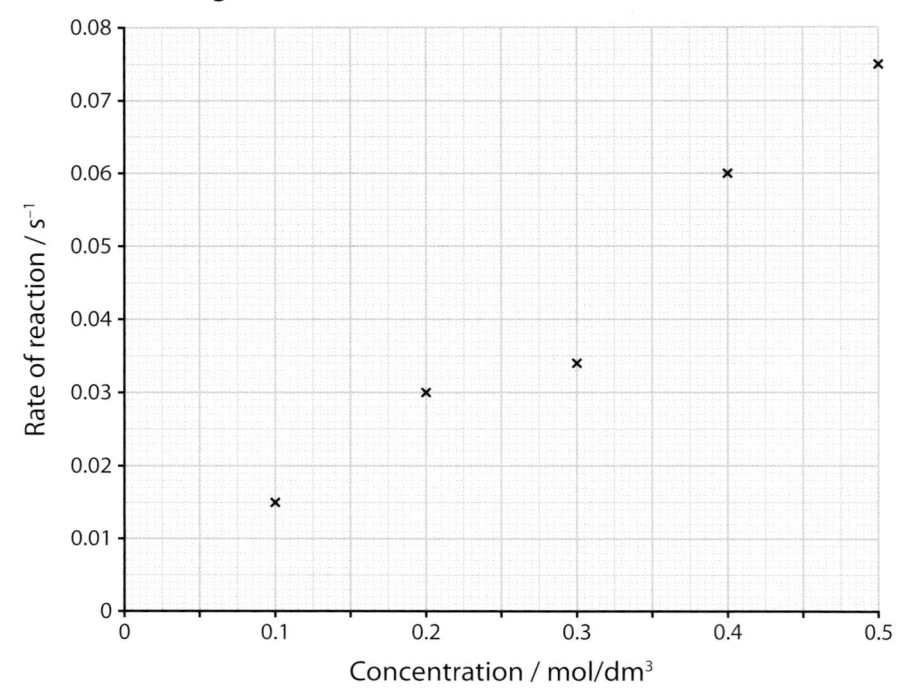

(a) Draw a **best fit line**. [2]
(b) (i) For which concentration of hydrochloric acid is there an anomaly? [1]
    (ii) What should be done to improve the experiment and remove this anomaly? [1]
(c) (i) Suggest how the time taken for the reaction to finish would have been determined. [1]
    (ii) Calculate the time taken for the reaction to finish for 0.1 mol/dm³ hydrochloric acid. [2]
(d) (i) State the trend shown in the results. [1]
    (ii) State two controlled variables during this experiment. [2]
    (iii) What is the independent variable in this experiment? [1]
    (iv) What is the dependent variable in this experiment? [1]

2.4 Equilibrium

1. A general reaction is shown below:

    $$2A(g) + B(g) \rightleftharpoons C(g) \qquad \text{Energy change} = +125 \text{ kJ}$$

    The symbols A, B and C do not represent symbols for elements.

    (a) Explain how an increase in temperature would affect the yield of C. [3]
    (b) Explain how an increase in pressure would affect the yield of C. [3]

2. For the reaction below:

    $$CH_4(g) + H_2O(g) \rightleftharpoons CO(g) + 3H_2(g)$$

    (a) What is meant by $\rightleftharpoons$? [1]
    (b) Explain why the reaction is described as a homogeneous equilibrium. [2]
    (c) How would the yield of hydrogen be affected if the pressure is increased? Explain your answer. [3]
    (d) How would a catalyst affect the position of equilibrium? [1]
    (e) The reaction is described as a dynamic equilibrium in a closed system.
      (i) What is meant by a dynamic equilibrium? [2]
      (ii) What is meant by a closed system? [1]

3. Ammonia reacts with oxygen to form nitrogen and water. The reaction is reversible.

    (a) Write a balanced symbol equation for the reversible reaction. [3]
    (b) Ammonia also reacts with oxygen to form nitrogen monoxide and water according to the equation below.

    $$4NH_3(g) + 5O_2(g) \rightleftharpoons 4NO(g) + 6H_2O(g)$$

    The energy change for this reaction is −905 kJ. A platinum/rhodium catalyst is used.
      (i) Explain how the yield of nitrogen monoxide would change if the temperature is increased. [3]
      (ii) Explain how the yield of nitrogen monoxide would change if the pressure is increased. [3]
      (iii) What effect does the catalyst have on the yield of nitrogen monoxide? [1]

4. The graph shown on the next page shows the percentage yield of ammonia at different temperatures and pressures in the Haber process. The equation for the Haber Process is:

    $$N_2(g) + 3H_2(g) \rightleftharpoons 2NH_3(g)$$

    The energy change for the reaction is −92 kJ.

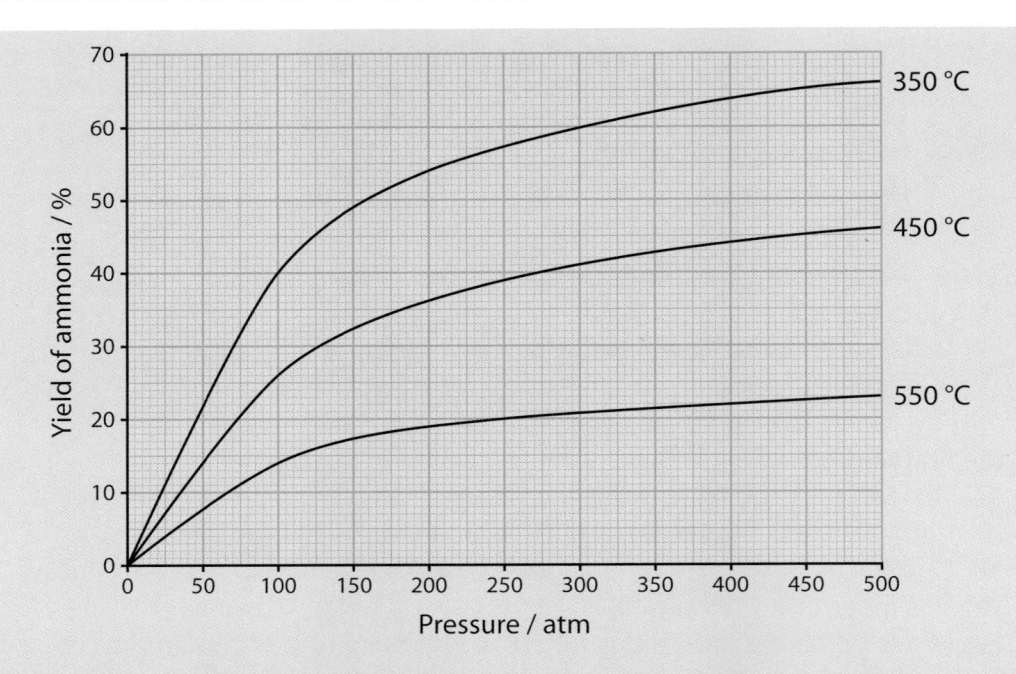

(a) State the trend in the yield of ammonia with increasing temperature. [1]
(b) State the trend in the yield of ammonia with increasing pressure. [1]
(c) State Le Châtelier's principle. [2]
(d) Use Le Châtelier's principle to explain the trend in (a). [2]
(e) Use Le Châtelier's principle to explain the trend in (b). [2]
(f) The industrial production of ammonia by the Haber process uses 200 atm and 450 °C.
  (i) What percentage yield of ammonia is obtained under these conditions? [1]
  (ii) Explain why the industrial production uses these conditions when a higher percentage yield of ammonia could be obtained using a higher pressure and a lower temperature. [2]

5. The reaction of hydrogen with iodine may be represented by the following equation:

$$H_2(g) + I_2(s) \rightleftharpoons 2HI(g)$$

The energy change for this reaction is +52.1 kJ.

(a) Explain whether this reaction is exothermic or endothermic. [1]
(b) Tick the boxes below which are correct for this reaction.

A catalyst would have no effect on the yield of hydrogen iodide	☐
The equilibrium is homogeneous	☐
An increase in temperature would increase the yield of hydrogen iodide	☐
A decrease in temperature would increase the yield of hydrogen iodide	☐

[2]

2.4 EQUILIBRIUM

6. Four reversible reactions are shown in the table below.

Reaction	Equation	Energy change (kJ)	Catalyst
A	$C_2H_4(g) + H_2O(g) \rightleftharpoons C_2H_5OH(g)$	−45	phosphoric acid
B	$2SO_2(g) + O_2(g) \rightleftharpoons 2SO_3(g)$	−196	vanadium(V) oxide
C	$N_2(g) + 3H_2(g) \rightleftharpoons 2NH_3(g)$	−92	iron
D	$N_2O_4(g) \rightleftharpoons 2NO_2(g)$	+59	none

(a) Explain why reaction A uses a high pressure to increase the yield of C_2H_5OH. [2]
(b) In which reactions (A, B, C, D), if any, would an increase in temperature move the position of equilibrium to the right? [1]
(c) Explain why reaction B uses a temperature of 450 °C when a higher yield of SO_3 would be obtained at a lower temperature. [1]
(d) Explain why reaction D is described as a homogeneous equilibrium. [2]
(e) Explain why a catalyst is important in the Haber process (reaction C) even though it has no effect on the percentage yield of ammonia. [1]

7. The diagrams below show two closed systems. Both systems contain hydrogen bromide at 450 °C which decomposes to form hydrogen and bromine.

$$2HBr(g) \rightleftharpoons H_2(g) + Br_2(g) \quad \text{Energy change} = +145 \text{ kJ}$$

Hydrogen bromide reacts with sodium hydroxide solution to form sodium bromide and water.

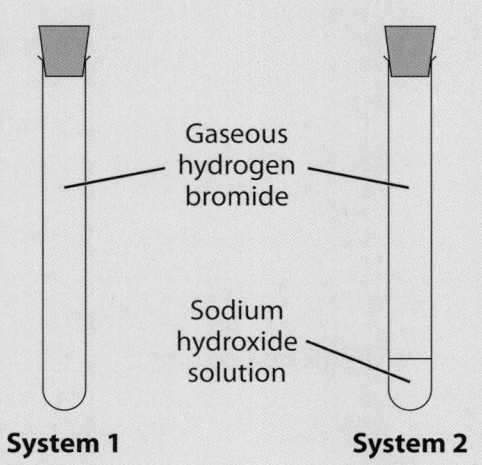

System 1: Gaseous hydrogen bromide

System 2: Gaseous hydrogen bromide, Sodium hydroxide solution

(a) Write a balanced symbol equation for hydrogen bromide reacting with sodium hydroxide. [2]
(b) Gaseous bromine is red–brown. Hydrogen gas and hydrogen bromide gas are colourless. Explain why system 2 would appear as a paler red–brown colour than system 1. [4]

2.5 Organic Chemistry

1. Organic compounds are grouped into homologous series. Alkanes and alkenes are homologous series of hydrocarbons. Alkanes do not have a functional group whereas alkenes do.

   (a) What is meant by the term homologous series? [3]
   (b) What is meant by the term hydrocarbon? [1]
   (c) State the functional groups present in alkenes. [1]
   (d) What is meant by a functional group? [1]
   (e) Write the general formula for the alkanes. [1]
   (f) Complete the table below.

Name	Molecular formula	Structural formula	State at room temperature
ethane			gas
	C_3H_6		
		H-C-C-C-C-H (with H's)	

   [4]

2. The structural formula for an organic compound is shown below.

   C=C-C-C-H (with H's)

   (a) Write the molecular formula of this compound. [1]
   (b) To which homologous series does this compound belong? [1]
   (c) Name this compound. [1]
   (d) What would be observed if this compound was mixed with bromine water? [2]
   (e) Name all the products of incomplete combustion of this compound. [3]
   (f) Draw the structural formula of another compound which has the same molecular formula as the one shown. Name the compound. [2]

2.5 ORGANIC CHEMISTRY

3. Crude oil is a finite resource and is the main industrial source of hydrocarbons. The process used to separate crude oil into simpler mixtures of hydrocarbons is shown in the diagram below.

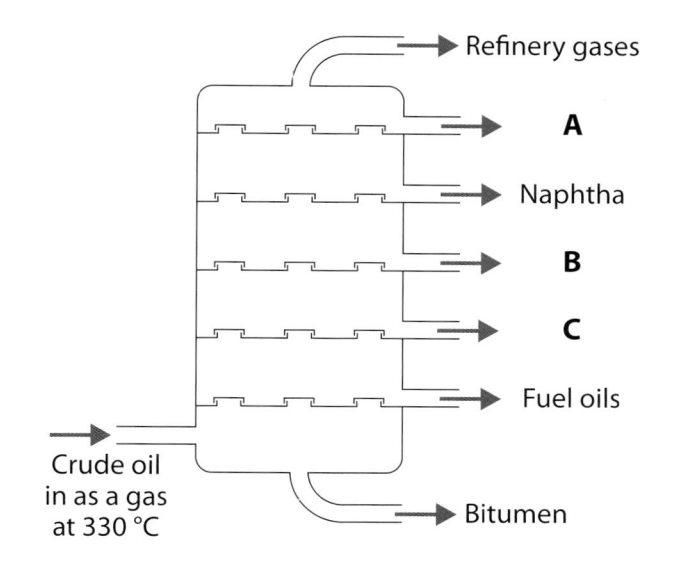

(a) Name the process shown in the diagram. [2]
(b) What labels should be placed at A, B and C on the diagram? [3]
(c) What is meant by a finite resource? [1]
(d) State one use of naphtha and one use of bitumen. [2]
(e) The refinery gases are used as fuels and contain alkanes with 1, 2, 3 and 4 carbon atoms.
  (i) What is the general formula of the alkanes? [1]
  (ii) Write the formula for the alkane with 3 carbon atoms and name this alkane. [2]
  (iii) Write a balanced symbol equation for the complete combustion of the alkane with 1 carbon atom. [3]

4. Hydrocarbons undergo combustion and are used as fuels. Octane is a component of petrol and is an alkane containing 8 carbon atoms. Butane is used in bottled gases.

(a) What is meant by the term fuel? [3]
(b) Using the general formula for alkanes, write the molecular formula of octane. [1]
(c) Write a balanced symbol equation for the complete combustion of butane. [3]
(d) Explain why butane is described as being saturated. [1]
(e) Name one alkene which would react with hydrogen to form butane. [1]
(f) In which fraction from the fractional distillation of crude oil would you find butane? [1]
(g) Incomplete combustion of hydrocarbons produces a toxic product. Name the toxic product. [1]

FURTHER CHEMICAL REACTIONS, RATES AND EQUILIBRIUM, CALCULATIONS AND ORGANIC CHEMISTRY

5. The structural formulae for six different organic compounds are shown below, labelled A, B, C, D, E and F.

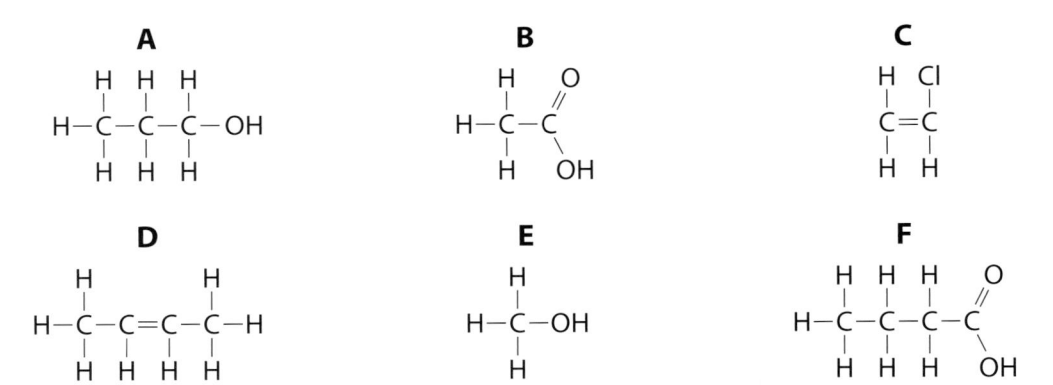

A
```
  H  H  H
  |  |  |
H-C--C--C-OH
  |  |  |
  H  H  H
```

B
```
  H   O
  |   ‖
H-C---C
  |    \
  H    OH
```

C
```
  H   Cl
  |   |
  C = C
  |   |
  H   H
```

D
```
  H      H
  |      |
H-C--C=C--C-H
  |  |  |  |
  H  H  H  H
```

E
```
  H
  |
H-C-OH
  |
  H
```

F
```
  H  H  H   O
  |  |  |   ‖
H-C--C--C--C
  |  |  |   \
  H  H  H   OH
```

(a) Which of the compounds (A, B, C, D, E and F) are hydrocarbons? [1]
(b) Which of the compounds (A, B, C, D, E and F) are unsaturated? [1]
(c) Which of the compounds (A, B, C, D, E and F) react with acidified potassium dichromate solution? [1]
(d) Which of the compounds (A, B, C, D, E and F) react with magnesium ribbon? [1]
(e) Name the compounds. [6]
(f) Compound C can form a polymer.
   (i) What type of polymerisation reaction occurs when C forms a polymer? [1]
   (ii) Write a structural equation for the formation of the polymer. [3]
   (iii) Name the polymer formed from C. [1]
   (iv) C undergoes incomplete combustion to form carbon monoxide, water and hydrogen chloride. Write a balanced symbol equation for this reaction. [3]

6. Hexane, C_6H_{14}, can undergo cracking to form butane and one other product.

(a) Write a balanced symbol equation for the cracking of hexane. [2]
(b) Name the other product. [1]
(c) Explain why cracking is important economically. [2]

7. Ethane is part of the refinery gases. Complete combustion of ethane produces carbon dioxide and water. Carbon dioxide contributes to the greenhouse effect.

(a) Write a balanced symbol equation for the complete combustion of ethane. [3]
(b) What chemical is used to test for carbon dioxide and what is the expected result? [3]
(c) State a chemical test for water and the expected result. [3]
(d) State two environmental problems caused by increased carbon dioxide levels in the atmosphere. [2]

2.5 ORGANIC CHEMISTRY

8. The reaction scheme below shows a series of reactions of ethene. (Double Award Chemistry candidates do not answer questions about reaction 2).

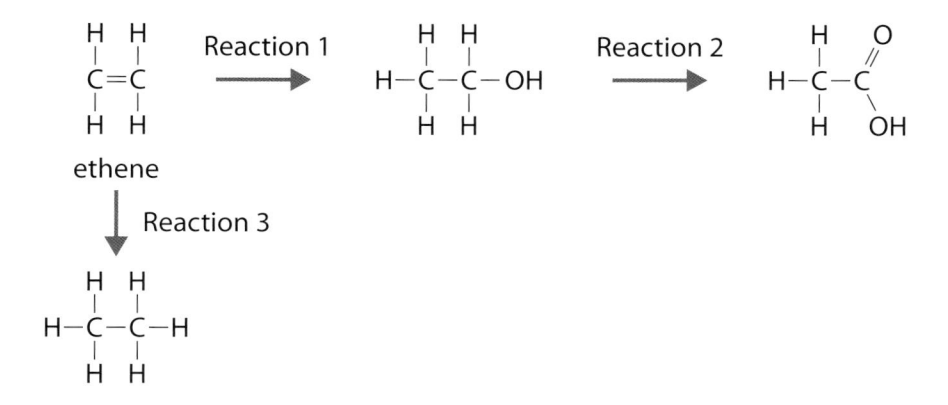

   (a) State the reagent required for each reaction. [3]
   (b) What type of reaction is occurring in reaction 2? [1]
   (c) Name the products of each reaction. [3]
   (d) Ethene also undergoes a polymerisation reaction.
       (i)   Draw the structure of the polymer formed from ethene. [1]
       (ii) What is the name of the polymer? [1]
       (iii) State two methods of disposal of polymers. [2]

9. The following organic reactions occur.

   Reaction A   methanol → methanoic acid

   Reaction B   ethanol + oxygen → carbon dioxide + water

   Reaction C   propene + bromine → 1,2–dibromopropane

   (a)
       (i)   What type of reaction is occurring in reaction A? [1]
       (ii) State the reagent used for reaction A and the colour change observed during the reaction. [2]
       (iii) Draw the structural formula of methanoic acid. [1]
   (b) (i)   Write a balanced symbol equation for reaction B. [3]
       (iii) Reaction B is a combustion reaction. Describe the appearance of the flame during this reaction. [1]
   (c) (i)   In reaction C, propene reacts with bromine in bromine water. What colour change is observed during this reaction? [2]
       (ii) Write the molecular formula for propene. [1]
       (iii) Draw a structural formula for 1,2–dibromopropane. [1]
       (iv) Explain why propene is described as unsaturated. [1]

FURTHER CHEMICAL REACTIONS, RATES AND EQUILIBRIUM, CALCULATIONS AND ORGANIC CHEMISTRY

10. The table below shows some organic compounds. Complete the table.

Name	Molecular formula	Structural formula	State at room temperature and pressure
methane		H–C(H)(H)–H (with H above and below)	
propane			gas
	C_4H_{10}		gas
	C_3H_6		gas
		H–C=C–C–C–H (with H's)	gas
		H–C–C=C–C–H (with H's)	gas
		H–C(H)(H)–OH	liquid
propan–1–ol			liquid
		H–C–C–C–H with OH on middle C	liquid
	C_3H_7COOH	H–C–C–C–C(=O)OH with H's	

[10]

2.5 ORGANIC CHEMISTRY

11. A section of a polymer is shown below.

$$-\underset{\underset{H}{|}}{\overset{\overset{CH_3}{|}}{C}}-\underset{\underset{CH_3}{|}}{\overset{\overset{H}{|}}{C}}-\underset{\underset{H}{|}}{\overset{\overset{CH_3}{|}}{C}}-\underset{\underset{CH_3}{|}}{\overset{\overset{H}{|}}{C}}-\underset{\underset{H}{|}}{\overset{\overset{CH_3}{|}}{C}}-\underset{\underset{CH_3}{|}}{\overset{\overset{H}{|}}{C}}-$$

(a) What is meant by the term polymer? [1]
(b) Draw the structure of the alkene monomer from which the polymer was formed and name the monomer. [2]
(c) State the type of reaction which occurred to form this polymer. [1]
(d) Describe the advantages and disadvantages of landfill and incineration for polymer disposal. [4]

12. (a) Ethanol may be prepared from ethene or by fermentation. Ethanol is an alcohol.
  (i) Describe the process of fermentation. Your answer should include the reactants, conditions and products.
  In this question, you will be assessed on the quality of your written communication including the use of specialist scientific terms. [6]
  (ii) Write a balanced symbol equation for the formation of ethanol from ethene. [2]
  (iii) Write the general formulae of the alcohols. [1]
  (iv) What colour change is observed when ethanol is warmed with acidified potassium dichromate solution? [1]
(b) Two alcohols have the molecular formula C_3H_7OH. Draw the structural formulae of the alcohols and name them. [4]
(c) Methanol can undergo combustion. Combustion may be described as complete or incomplete.
  (i) Write a balanced symbol equation for the complete combustion of methanol. [3]
  (ii) What are the conditions required for incomplete combustion? [1]
  (iii) Name the toxic product formed when incomplete combustion occurs and explain its toxic effect on the human body. [3]

13. The table below shows some carboxylic acids. Carboxylic acids are weak acids and they react with metals, metal carbonates and metal hydroxides forming salts.

Name	Molecular formula	Structural formula	State at room temperature
propanoic acid		H-C(H)(H)-C(H)(H)-C(=O)-OH	
	HCOOH		
ethanoic acid			
	C_3H_7COOH		

(a) Complete the table. [4]
(b) What is meant by the term weak acid? [1]
(c) Write a balanced symbol equation for the reaction of C_3H_7COOH with magnesium. [3]
(d) Name the salt formed when HCOOH reacts with sodium hydroxide. [1]
(e) Write a balanced symbol equation for the reaction of ethanoic acid with calcium carbonate. [3]
(f) Solid copper(II) carbonate reacts with propanoic acid. Effervescence is observed as carbon dioxide gas is produced and the reaction releases heat.
　(i)　Write a balanced symbol equation for this reaction. [3]
　(ii)　Describe how you would test for carbon dioxide gas including the result for a positive test. [3]
　(iii)　What other observations would be made during this reaction? [3]

2.5 ORGANIC CHEMISTRY

14. The following results were obtained when four different unknown organic compounds labelled W, X, Y and Z were tested as shown below.

Test	W	X	Y	Z
Mix the compound with bromine water	orange solution changes to colourless	solution remains orange	solution remains orange	solution remains orange
Mix with compound with acidified potassium dichromate solution and warm in a water bath	solution remains orange	orange solution changes to green	solution remains orange	solution remains orange
Add magnesium ribbon to a solution of the compound	no reaction	no reaction	fizzing magnesium disappears heat released	no reaction

(a) Which compound (W, X, Y or Z) is an alkane? [1]
(b) To which homologous series does compound W belong? [1]
(c) Which compound contains the carboxyl functional group? [1]
(d) Which compound could be propan–1–ol? [1]
(e) Fizzing is observed when magnesium reacts with compound Y as a gas is produced.
 (i) Name the gas produced when magnesium reacts with compound Y. [1]
 (ii) Describe how you would test for the gas produced in this reaction. [2]

15. Many atmospheric pollutants are produced during the combustion of fossil fuels such as soot, carbon monoxide and sulfur dioxide.
(a) State one negative effect of the presence of soot in the atmosphere. [1]
(b) Explain how carbon monoxide is produced during the combustion of fossil fuels. [1]
(c) Sulfur impurities in fossil fuels lead to the production of sulfur dioxide when the fuels undergo combustion. Sulfur dioxide reacts with water to form acid rain.
(d) (i) Write a balanced symbol equation for sulfur reacting with oxygen to form sulfur dioxide. [2]
 (ii) Write a balanced symbol equation for the formation of acid rain from sulfur dioxide. [2]
 (iii) State three harmful environmental effects of acid rain. [3]

2.6 Quantitative Chemistry

Making solutions

1. A solution of potassium hydroxide was prepared as described below.

   11.2 g of potassium hydroxide were dissolved in a small volume (approximately 50 cm³) of deionised water in a beaker. The solution was stirred with a glass rod. The glass rod was washed with deionised water before it was removed from the beaker.

   The solution was transferred to a 250 cm³ volumetric flask using a filter funnel. The beaker and the filter funnel were then rinsed with deionised water with all rinsings going into the volumetric flask.

   Deionised water was added to the flask until the bottom of the meniscus was on the line. The flask was stoppered and inverted.

   (a) State two practical ways in which loss of potassium hydroxide was prevented. [2]
   (b) Explain why a small volume of deionised water was used to dissolve the potassium hydroxide in the beaker. [1]
   (c) Why was the flask stoppered and inverted? [1]
   (d) Calculate the concentration of the solution in mol/dm³. [2]

2. Calculate the mass, in grams, of ammonium sulfate, $(NH_4)_2SO_4$, dissolved in 150 cm³ of deionised water to form a solution of concentration 0.12 mol.dm³. [2]

3. Calculate the volume, in cm³, of deionised water in which 5.18 g of solid magnesium nitrate, $Mg(NO_3)_2$, should be dissolved to form a solution of concentration 0.28 mol/dm³. [2]

4. Calcium hydroxide is sparingly soluble in water. A saturated solution at 20 °C has a concentration of 0.0234 mol/dm³.

   (a) What is the common name for calcium hydroxide solution? [1]
   (b) Calculate the mass, in grams, of calcium hydroxide, $Ca(OH)_2$, dissolved in 250 cm³ of a saturated solution at 20 °C. [2]

5. Complete the table below which shows different solutions containing different solutes. Calculate the missing quantities for each solution.

Solute	Mass of solute in the solution (g)	Moles of solute in the solution (mol)	Volume of the solution (cm³)	Concentration of the solution (mol/dm³)
NaOH	0.6	0.015	100	0.15
$CuCl_2$	32.4		250	
$Fe_2(SO_4)_3$	30			0.6
$Na_2CO_3.10H_2O$			225	0.2

[6]

2.6 QUANTITATIVE CHEMISTRY

Acid–base reactions/titrations

6. Sodium hydroxide solution reacts with hydrochloric acid according to the equation:

$$NaOH + HCl \rightarrow NaCl + H_2O$$

   25.0 cm³ of sodium hydroxide solution were placed in a conical flask with phenolphthalein indicator. 17.5 cm³ of 0.03 mol/dm³ hydrochloric acid were added to reach the end point.

   (a) Name the piece of apparatus used to place 25.0 cm³ of sodium hydroxide solution in the conical flask. [1]
   (b) Name the piece of apparatus used to measure the volume of the hydrochloric acid added. [1]
   (c) What is the colour changed observed at the end point? [2]
   (d) (i) Calculate the number of moles of hydrochloric acid which reacts. [1]
   (ii) Calculate the number of moles of sodium hydroxide present in 25.0 cm³ of the solution. [1]
   (iii) Calculate the concentration of the sodium hydroxide solution in mol/dm³. [1]

7. Aluminium hydroxide reacts with sulfuric acid according to the equation:

$$2Al(OH)_3 + 3H_2SO_4 \rightarrow Al_2(SO_4)_3 + 6H_2O$$

   Calculate the volume, in cm³, of 1.5 mol/dm³ sulfuric acid required to react with 6.24 g of solid aluminium hydroxide. [3]

8. 25.0 cm³ of a solution of sodium hydroxide were neutralised by a 22.5 cm³ of a solution of sulfuric acid of concentration 0.48 mol/dm³.

   The equation for the reaction is:

$$2NaOH + H_2SO_4 \rightarrow Na_2SO_4 + 2H_2O$$

   Calculate the concentration of the solution of sodium hydroxide in mol/dm³. [3]

9. Potassium hydroxide reacts with sulfuric acid according to the equation:

$$2KOH + H_2SO_4 \rightarrow K_2SO_4 + 2H_2O$$

   0.0085 moles of sulfuric acid reacts with 25.0 cm³ of potassium hydroxide solution.

   (a) Calculate the number of moles of potassium hydroxide which reacts with 0.0085 moles of sulfuric acid. [1]
   (b) Calculate the concentration of the potassium hydroxide solution in mol/dm³. [1]
   (c) Calculate the concentration of the potassium hydroxide solution in g/dm³. Give your answer to 1 decimal place. [1]

FURTHER CHEMICAL REACTIONS, RATES AND EQUILIBRIUM, CALCULATIONS AND ORGANIC CHEMISTRY

10. 25.0 cm³ of a 0.125 mol/dm³ solution of sodium hydroxide were placed in a conical flask with phenolphthalein indicator. The solution was titrated against a solution of hydrochloric acid of unknown concentration. The results of the titration are given in the table below.

	Initial burette reading (cm³)	Final burette reading (cm³)	Titre (cm³)
Rough titration	0.4	21.5	
First accurate titration	21.5	41.0	
Second accurate titration	22.8	42.3	

(a) State the colour change observed at the end point. [2]
(b) Complete the table. [1]
(c) Calculate the average titre and state its units. [2]
(d) The equation for the reaction is:

$$NaOH + HCl \rightarrow NaCl + H_2O$$

(i) Calculate the number of moles of sodium hydroxide present in the conical flask. [1]
(ii) Calculate the number of moles of hydrochloric acid added from the burette. [1]
(iii) Calculate the concentration of the hydrochloric acid in mol/dm³. Give your answer to 2 decimal places. [1]
(iv) Calculate the concentration of the hydrochloric acid in g/dm³. [1]

11. 10.0 cm³ of a solution of sodium hydroxide were diluted to 250 cm³ in a volumetric flask. 25.0 cm³ of the diluted solution were placed in a conical flask and titrated against a solution of ethanoic acid of concentration 0.08 mol/dm³ using phenolphthalein indicator. The conical flask was placed on a white tile during the titration. The end point was determined to be at 20.0 cm³.

(a) Explain why the conical flask was placed on a white tile. [1]
(b) State two ways in which accuracy would be ensured when determining the end point. [2]
(c) State the colour change at the end point. [2]
(d) The equation for the reaction is:

$$CH_3COOH + NaOH \rightarrow CH_3COONa + H_2O$$

(i) Calculate the number of moles of ethanoic acid added. [1]
(ii) Calculate the number of moles of sodium hydroxide present in 25.0 cm³ of the diluted solution. [1]
(iii) Calculate the concentration, in mol/dm³, of the diluted solution of sodium hydroxide. [1]
(iv) What is the dilution factor applied to the solution of sodium hydroxide? [1]
(v) Calculate the concentration, in mol/dm³, of the undiluted solution of sodium hydroxide. [1]

2.6 QUANTITATIVE CHEMISTRY

12. A solution of rubidium hydroxide contains 7.14 g of rubidium hydroxide in 100 cm³ of deionised water.

    (a) Calculate the concentration of the solution of rubidium hydroxide in g/dm³ [1]
    (b) Calculate the concentration of the solution of rubidium hydroxide in mol/dm³. [1]
    (c) 25.0 cm³ of the solution of rubidium hydroxide were placed in a conical flask and titrated against sulfuric acid using methyl orange indicator.

The equation for the reaction is:

$$2RbOH + H_2SO_4 \rightarrow Rb_2SO_4 + 2H_2O$$

The table below gives the results of the titration.

	Titration 1	Titration 2	Titration 3	Titration 4
Final burette reading (cm³)	15.2	29.1	43.8	44.3
Initial burette reading (cm³)	0.0	15.2	29.1	30.2
Titre (cm³)	15.2	13.9	14.7	14.1

    (i) State the colour change observed at the end point. [2]
    (ii) Which two titrations are reliable? [1]
    (iii) Calculate the average titre using the results of the titres you identified in **(c)(ii)** above. State the units. [2]
    (iv) Calculate the concentration of the solution of sulfuric acid in mol/dm³. [3]
    (v) Calculate the concentration of the solution of sulfuric acid in g/dm³. [1]

13. A solution was prepared by dissolving 9.45 g of hydrated barium hydroxide, $Ba(OH)_2 \cdot 8H_2O$, in 1000 cm³ of deionised water. 25.0 cm³ of this solution were pipetted into a conical flask and titrated against 0.02 mol/dm³ hydrochloric acid.

The balanced symbol equation for the reaction is:

$$Ba(OH)_2 + 2HCl \rightarrow BaCl_2 + 2H_2O$$

    (a) Describe how the pipette was prepared and used safely to transfer 25.0 cm³ of the barium hydroxide solution into a conical flask.
    In this question, you will be assessed on the quality of your written communication including the use of specialist scientific terms. [6]
    (b) Calculate the volume of hydrochloric acid, in cm³, required to react with 25.0 cm³ of the barium hydroxide in the solution. [4]

FURTHER CHEMICAL REACTIONS, RATES AND EQUILIBRIUM, CALCULATIONS AND ORGANIC CHEMISTRY

Determining formula

14. 2.07 g of an unknown metal carbonate, M_2CO_3, were dissolved in deionised water and the volume made up to 100 cm³ in a volumetric flask. 25.0 cm³ of the solution were titrated against 0.6 mol/dm³ hydrochloric acid using methyl orange. The average titre was found to be 12.5 cm³.

(a) State the colour change at the end point. [2]
(b) The balanced symbol equation for the reaction may be represented as:

$$M_2CO_3 + 2HCl \rightarrow 2MCl + CO_2 + H_2O$$

(i) Calculate the number of moles of hydrochloric acid which reacted. [1]
(ii) Calculate the number of moles of M_2CO_3 present in 25.0 cm³ of the solution. [1]
(iii) Calculate the number of moles of M_2CO_3 present in 100 cm³ of the solution. [1]
(iv) Calculate the relative formula mass (M_r) of M_2CO_3. [1]
(v) Calculate the relative atomic mass (A_r) of M and state the identity of M. [2]

15. 5.34 g of a sample of hydrated sodium carbonate, $Na_2CO_3.xH_2O$ were dissolved in deionised water and transferred to a 250 cm³ volumetric flask. The volume was made up using deionised water. 25.0 cm³ of this solution were titrated against 0.15 mol/dm³ hydrochloric acid and 40.0 cm³ of the acid were required. The equation for the reaction is:

$$Na_2CO_3 + 2HCl \rightarrow 2NaCl + CO_2 + H_2O$$

(a) Calculate the number of moles of hydrochloric acid used. [1]
(b) Calculate the number of moles of Na_2CO_3 present in 25.0 cm³ of the solution. [1]
(c) Calculate the number of moles of Na_2CO_3 present in 250 cm³ of the solution. [1]
(d) Calculate the relative formula mass (M_r) of $Na_2CO_3.xH_2O$ using the initial mass and the answer to **(c)**. [1]
(e) Calculate the value of x in $Na_2CO_3.xH_2O$. [1]

16. 4.0 g of an unknown insoluble metal oxide, MO, were reacted with 40.0 cm³ of 2 mol/dm³ nitric acid. After the reaction was complete the leftover oxide was filtered and dried. 0.8 g of the oxide remained. The equation for the reaction may be represented as:

$$MO + 2HNO_3 \rightarrow M(NO_3)_2 + H_2O$$

(a) Suggest why nitric acid was used instead of hydrochloric acid or sulfuric acid. [1]
(b) Calculate the mass of the metal oxide, MO, which reacted. [1]
(c) (i) Calculate the number of moles of nitric acid used. [1]
(ii) Calculate the number of moles of MO which reacted with the nitric acid. [1]
(iii) Using your answer to **(b)** and **(c)(ii)**, calculate the relative formula mass (M_r) of the metal oxide. [1]
(iv) Calculate the relative atomic mass (A_r) of M and use it to identify M. [2]

2.6 QUANTITATIVE CHEMISTRY

17. A solution containing 8.68 g of hydrated rubidium carbonate, $Rb_2CO_3 \cdot xH_2O$, was made up in 100 cm³ of deionised water. A 25.0 cm³ sample of this solution was titrated against 1.25 mol/dm³ hydrochloric acid. 14.0 cm³ of the acid were required to reach the end point. The equation for the reaction is:

$$Rb_2CO_3 + 2HCl \rightarrow 2RbCl + CO_2 + H_2O$$

(a) Calculate the number of moles of hydrochloric acid used. [1]
(b) Calculate the number of moles of Rb_2CO_3 in 25.0 cm³ of the solution. [1]
(c) Calculate the number of moles of Rb_2CO_3 in 100 cm³ of the solution. [1]
(d) Calculate the mass, in grams, of anhydrous rubidium carbonate, Rb_2CO_3, present in 100 cm³ of the solution. [1]
(e) Calculate the mass, in grams, of water present in the solid sample of $Rb_2CO_3 \cdot xH_2O$. [1]
(f) Calculate the number of moles of water present in the solid sample of $Rb_2CO_3 \cdot xH_2O$. [1]
(g) Using your answers to (c) and (f) determine the value of x in $Rb_2CO_3 \cdot xH_2O$. [1]

18. 5.13 g of an unknown soluble Group 2 hydroxide, $M(OH)_2$, were dissolved in deionised water and transferred to a volumetric flask. The volume was made up to 100 cm³ using deionised water.

A 25.0 cm³ sample of this solution was pipetted into a conical flask and 3 drops of methyl orange were added. Four conical flasks were prepared in this way.

A burette was prepared and filled with 0.40 mol/dm³ sulfuric acid. A rough titration and three subsequent titrations were carried out. The results of the titrations are shown in the table below.

The equation for the reaction may be represented as:

$$M(OH)_2 + H_2SO_4 \rightarrow MSO_4 + 2H_2O$$

	Rough titration	Titration 1	Titration 2	Titration 3
Initial burette reading (cm³)	0.2	19.6	0.5	18.0
Final burette reading (cm³)	19.8	38.3	18.5	36.8
Titre (cm³)	19.6	18.7	18.0	18.8

(a) State the colour change observed at the end point. [2]
(b) Describe how the burette is prepared for use in this titration. [4]
(c) Explain why a rough titration is carried out. [1]
(d) Explain why the results of titration 1 and titration 3 are the reliable results which will be used to calculate the average titre. [1]
(e) State two ways in which the end point may be determined accurately. [2]
(f) Calculate the average titre **using only the results of titration 1 and titration 3** and state the units. [2]
(g) (i) Using the average titre from (f), calculate the number of moles of sulfuric acid used. [1]
    (ii) Calculate the number of moles of $M(OH)_2$ present in 25.0 cm³ of the solution. [1]
    (iii) Calculate the number of moles of $M(OH)_2$ present in 100 cm³ of the solution. [1]

(iv) Calculate the relative formula mass (M_r) of M(OH)$_2$ using the initial mass and the answer to **(g)(iii)** above. [1]

(v) Calculate the relative atomic mass (A_r) of M and use it to identify M. [1]

(h) The titration was repeated using a different soluble Group 2 metal hydroxide. 2.44 g of the solid metal hydroxide were dissolved in 100 cm³ of deionised water and 25.0 cm³ of this solution required 12.5 cm³ of 0.40 mol/dm³ sulfuric acid. Determine the identity of the metal in this metal hydroxide. **Show all your working out.** [6]

Gas volumes and Avogadro's Law

19. Hydrogen gas is formed when aluminium powder reacts with hydrochloric acid. The balanced symbol equation for the reaction is:

$$2Al(s) + 6HCl(aq) \rightarrow 2AlCl_3(aq) + 3H_2(g)$$

0.54 g of aluminium powder reacted with an excess of 2.0 mol/dm³ hydrochloric acid.

(a) Calculate the number of moles of aluminium used. [1]
(b) Calculate the number of moles of hydrogen formed. [1]
(c) Calculate the volume, in dm³, of hydrogen gas formed at 20 °C and 1 atm pressure. [1]
(d) Calculate the minimum volume, in cm³, of 2.0 mol/dm³ hydrochloric acid required to react with all of the aluminium. [2]

20. Calcium reacts with oxygen gas according to the balanced symbol equation.

$$2Ca(s) + O_2(g) \rightarrow 2CaO(s)$$

Calculate the volume, in cm³, of oxygen gas required to react with 0.12 g of calcium. [3]

21. Iron reacts with chlorine gas forming iron(III) chloride. The equation for the reaction is:

$$2Fe(s) + 3Cl_2(g) \rightarrow 2FeCl_3(s)$$

Calculate the mass, in grams, of iron required to react with 0.18 dm³ of chlorine gas. [3]

22. Silver nitrate decomposes when heated as shown by the equation:

$$2AgNO_3(s) \rightarrow 2Ag(s) + 2NO_2(g) + O_2(g)$$

7.65 g of silver nitrate were heated until all of it decomposed.

(a) Explain how you would ensure that all of the silver nitrate had decomposed. [1]
(b) (i) Calculate the number of moles of silver nitrate used. [1]
    (ii) Calculate the total number of moles of gas formed. [1]
    (iii) Calculate the total volume, in cm³, of gas formed at 20 °C and 1 atm pressure. [1]

2.6 QUANTITATIVE CHEMISTRY

23. 0.3 g of hydrated magnesium carbonate, $MgCO_3.xH_2O$, were reacted with 20.0 cm³ of 1.0 mol/dm³ hydrochloric acid (an excess). 60 cm³ of carbon dioxide gas were produced.

(a) Name the piece of apparatus used to measure the volume of carbon dioxide gas produced. [1]

(b) The equation for the reaction is:

$$MgCO_3 + 2HCl \rightarrow MgCl_2 + CO_2 + H_2O$$

(i) Calculate the number of moles of carbon dioxide gas produced. [1]
(ii) Calculate the number of moles of $MgCO_3$ which reacted with the hydrochloric acid. [1]
(iii) Calculate the mass, in grams, of $MgCO_3$ which reacted. [1]
(iv) Calculate the mass, in grams, of water present in $MgCO_3.xH_2O$. [1]
(v) Calculate the number of moles of water present in $MgCO_3.xH_2O$. [1]
(vi) Using your answers to (ii) and (v) above, determine the value of x in $MgCO_3.xH_2O$. [1]

24. Nitrogen monoxide, NO, reacts with oxygen to form nitrogen dioxide. The balanced symbol equation for the reaction is:

$$2NO(g) + O_2(g) \rightarrow 2NO_2(g)$$

(a) State Avogadro's Law. [2]

(b) Using Avogadro's Law calculate the volume of oxygen, in cm³, required to react with 50 cm³ of nitrogen monoxide. [1]

(c) 50 cm³ of nitrogen monoxide was mixed with 100 cm³ of oxygen (an excess). The reaction was complete when all of the nitrogen monoxide was used up.
(i) Calculate the volume, in cm³, of oxygen left over when the reaction was complete. [1]
(ii) Calculate the volume, in cm³, of nitrogen dioxide formed in this reaction. [1]

25. Ammonia reacts with oxygen according to the equation:

$$4NH_3(g) + 3O_2(g) \rightarrow 2N_2(g) + 6H_2O(l)$$

(a) Calculate the volume, in dm³, of oxygen required to react with 20 dm³ of ammonia. [1]
(b) If a mixture of 150 cm³ of ammonia and 150 cm³ of oxygen were allowed to react, all of the ammonia is used up.
(i) Calculate the volume, in cm³, of oxygen left over. [2]
(ii) Calculate the volume, in cm³, of nitrogen formed. [1]
(iii) The total volume of gas at the start of the reaction was 300 cm³. Calculate the total volume of gas remaining when the reaction is complete at 20 °C. [1]

FURTHER CHEMICAL REACTIONS, RATES AND EQUILIBRIUM, CALCULATIONS AND ORGANIC CHEMISTRY

Atom Economy

26. Copper may be produced in phytomining and also from a solid ore containing the copper compound Cu_2S.

(a) In phytomining, copper may be produced by a displacement reaction using iron. The balanced symbol equation is:

$$CuSO_4(aq) + Fe(s) \rightarrow Cu(s) + FeSO_4(aq)$$

    (i) Write an expression for atom economy. [1]
    (ii) Calculate the atom economy of this reaction. Give your answer to 1 decimal place. [2]

(b) Copper may be produced from its ore by the reaction below:

$$Cu_2S(s) + O_2(g) \rightarrow 2Cu(s) + SO_2(g)$$

Calculate the atom economy for this reaction. Give your answer to 1 decimal place. [2]

(c) Explain which process (phytomining or production from its ore) has the least waste. [1]

27. The balanced symbol equations for four reactions are given below, labelled A, B, C and D.

Reaction A: $Fe_2O_3 + 3CO \rightarrow 2Fe + 3CO_2$

Reaction B: $C_6H_{12}O_6 \rightarrow 2C_2H_5OH + 2CO_2$

Reaction C: $NH_3 + HCl \rightarrow NH_4Cl$

Reaction D: $2H_2O_2 \rightarrow 2H_2O + O_2$

(a) Which reaction (A, B, C or D) has 100 % atom economy? [1]

(b) Calculate the atom economy of reaction B if C_2H_5OH is the desired product. Give your answer to 1 decimal place. [2]

(c) $C_6H_{12}O_6$ is the chemical formula for glucose, a simple sugar. Suggest what process is shown by the equation for Reaction B. [1]

2.7 Electrochemistry

1. The diagram below shows the apparatus used to carry out the electrolysis of molten lithium chloride in a crucible.

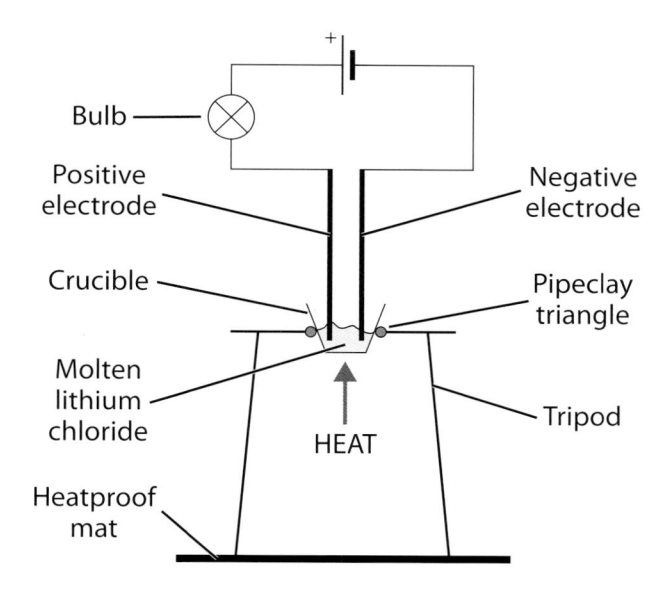

   (a) What is meant by the term electrolysis? [2]
   (b) What name is used for the negative electrode? [1]
   (c) Explain why molten lithium chloride conducts electricity. [1]
   (d) What term is used to describe a liquid which conducts electricity and is decomposed by it? [1]
   (e) What is observed at the positive electrode? [2]
   (f) Write a half equation for the reaction occurring at the negative electrode. [2]

2. Molten ionic compounds and acids conduct electricity. Metals and graphite also conduct electricity.

   (a) State any effect of the conduction of electricity on metals and on molten ionic compounds and explain how they conduct electricity. [3]
   (b) What is observed at the anode when molten lead(II) bromide conducts electricity? [2]
   (c) Name the gas produced at the cathode when dilute sulfuric acid conducts electricity. [1]
   (d) Write a half equation for the reaction which occurs at the cathode when molten lead(II) bromide conducts electricity. [3]
   (e) Suggest what would be observed at the anode when molten sodium iodide conducts electricity. [2]

FURTHER CHEMICAL REACTIONS, RATES AND EQUILIBRIUM, CALCULATIONS AND ORGANIC CHEMISTRY

3. Complete the table below which details the products formed and half equations for the electrolysis of some electrolytes. Some have been completed for you.

Electrolyte	Product(s) formed at the anode	Product(s) formed at the cathode	Half equation for reaction at anode	Half equation for reaction at cathode
Molten zinc chloride	[1]	zinc	[3]	[3]
Dilute sulfuric acid	oxygen and water	[1]	[3]	[3]
Molten sodium oxide	[1]	[1]	[3]	[2]
Molten lithium bromide	[1]	[1]	[3]	[2]

4. During the electrolysis of dilute sulfuric acid, hydrogen gas is produced at the cathode. A reduction reaction occurs at the cathode.
   (a) Explain why the reaction at the cathode may be described as reduction. [2]
   (b) Name the material which is used for the electrodes during the electrolysis of dilute sulfuric acid. [1]
   (c) What is observed at the anode? [2]
   (d) Write a half equation for the reaction which occurs at the anode. [3]
   (e) During the electrolysis 40 cm^3 of hydrogen gas were produced at the cathode. Predict the volume of gas produced at the anode. [1]

2.7 ELECTROLYSIS

5. Aluminium is extracted from its ore in the Hall–Héroult cell shown below.

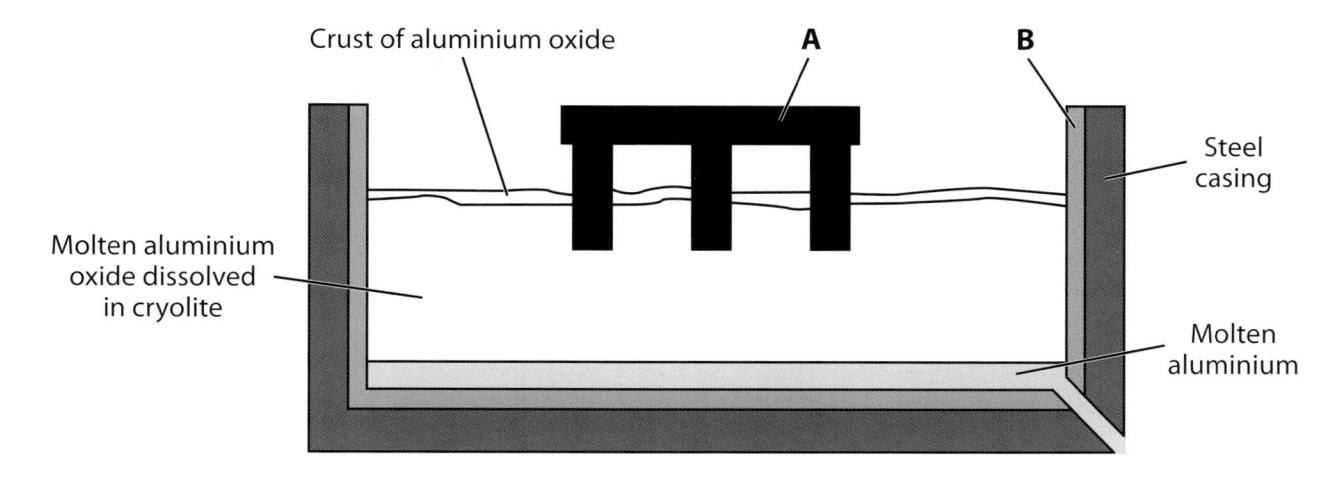

Labels on diagram: Crust of aluminium oxide; A; B; Steel casing; Molten aluminium oxide dissolved in cryolite; Molten aluminium

(a) Name the ore from which aluminium is extracted. [1]
(b) State two reasons why molten aluminium oxide is dissolved in molten cryolite. [2]
(c) State one benefit of the crust of aluminium oxide. [1]
(d) What is the operating temperature of the process? [1]
(e) What labels should be placed at A and B? [2]
(f) Write a half equation for the production of aluminium at B. [3]
(g) Write a half equation for the production of oxygen at A. [3]
(h) Explain why A has to be replaced periodically. Include a balanced symbol equation in your answer. [3]

6. Electrolysis of molten potassium chloride at 800 °C produces molten potassium and gaseous chlorine using graphite electrodes. The overall equation for the electrolysis is given below:

$$2KCl(l) \rightarrow 2K(l) + Cl_2(g)$$

(a) State two reasons why graphite is used as the material for the electrodes. [2]
(b) What is observed at the anode during this electrolysis? [2]
(c) Write a half equation for the reaction occurring at the cathode. [2]
(d) Explain why molten potassium chloride conducts electricity. [2]
(e) Calculate the volume, in cm³, of chlorine gas produced when 10.43 g of potassium chloride are electrolysed in this way and the gas collected at 20 °C and 1 atm pressure. [3]

FURTHER CHEMICAL REACTIONS, RATES AND EQUILIBRIUM, CALCULATIONS AND ORGANIC CHEMISTRY

7. The apparatus below may be used to carry out the electrolysis of dilute sulfuric acid and collect the gases produced.

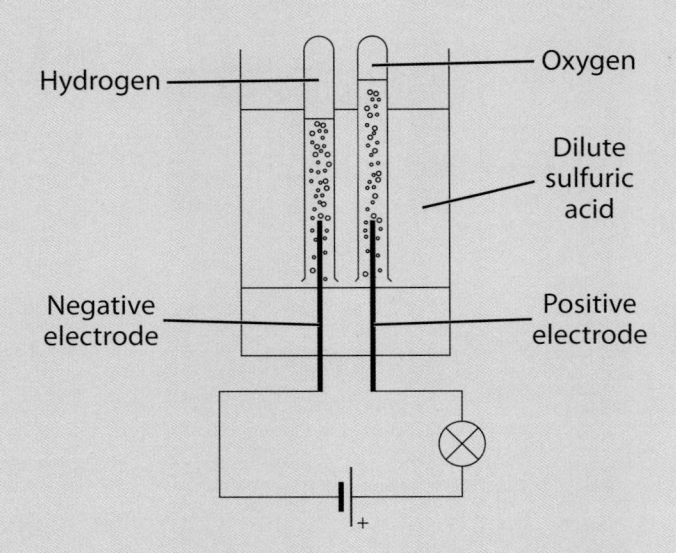

    (a) What names are given to the positive electrode and the negative electrode? [1]
    (b) Write a half equation for the reaction occurring at the negative electrode. [3]
    (c) Explain why the volume of hydrogen is twice the volume of oxygen. [2]
    (d) What material is used for the electrodes? [1]
    (e) Describe a test for hydrogen gas. [2]
    (f) A glowing splint was applied to the test tube of oxygen gas. What is observed? [1]

8. The diagram below shows the processes in the production of aluminium from its ore.

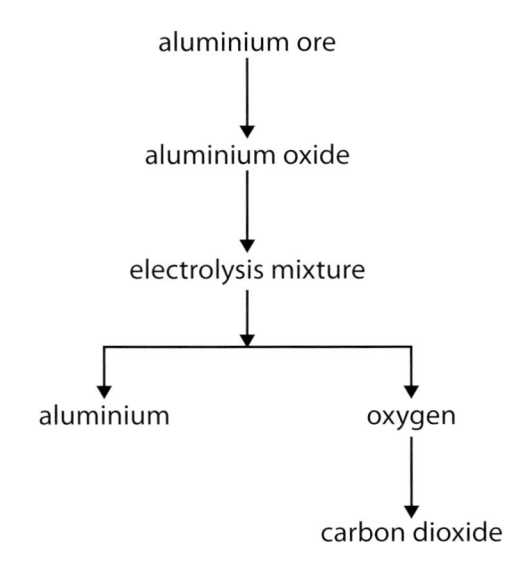

    (a) Name the ore of aluminium. [1]
    (b) Write a balanced symbol equation for the conversion of aluminium oxide into aluminium and oxygen. [3]
    (c) What is added to aluminium oxide to form the electrolysis mixture? [1]

(d) (i) Complete the table below for the production of aluminium and oxygen during the electrolysis.

Electrode	Electrolysis product	Half equation
Anode	[1]	[3]
Cathode	[1]	[3]

(ii) Explain why the reaction occurring at the anode is described as oxidation. [2]

(e) Explain how carbon dioxide is formed. [2]

(f) Explain why recycling aluminium is preferable to producing aluminium from its ore. [1]

2.8 Energy Changes in Chemistry

1. Hydrogen iodide may be decomposed into hydrogen gas and iodine gas in an endothermic reaction. The equation is:

   $$2HI(g) \rightarrow H_2(g) + I_2(g)$$

   (a) What colour is iodine gas? [1]
   (b) Explain, in terms of bonds, why this reaction is endothermic. [3]

2. Four chemical reactions are shown in the table below with their energy changes. They are labelled A, B, C and D.

Reaction	Equation	Energy change (kJ)	Endothermic	Exothermic
A	$C_2H_5OH + 3O_2 \rightarrow 2CO_2 + 3H_2O$	−1368		✓
B	$CaCO_3 \rightarrow CaO + CO_2$	+178		
C	$NaOH + HCl \rightarrow NaCl + H_2O$	−57		
D	$Zn + CuSO_4 \rightarrow ZnSO_4 + Cu$	−217		

   (a) Place a tick (✓) in the endothermic or endothermic column in the table for reactions B, C and D. [3]
   (b) Apart from exothermic or endothermic, what type of reaction is occurring for A, B, C and D? [4]
   (c) What is meant by the term exothermic? [1]
   (d) Explain, in terms of bonds, why reaction A is exothermic. [3]
   (e) Complete the reaction profile shown below for reaction A showing the energy level of the products, the energy change and draw a reaction pathway labelling the activation energy. [4]

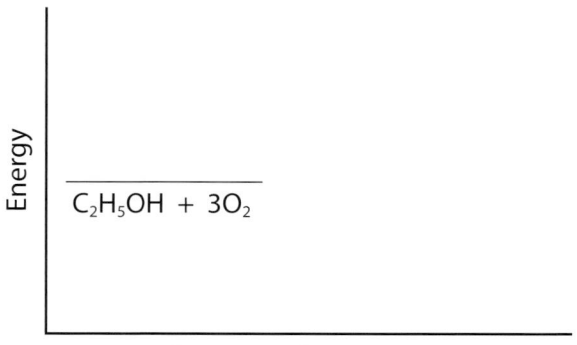

2.8 ENERGY CHANGES IN CHEMISTRY

3. The table below gives some bond energy values.

Bond	Bond energy (kJ)
C–H	412
O–H	463
O=O	496
C=C	611
C=O	803

Ethene reacts with oxygen to form carbon dioxide and water.
The equation for the reaction is:

$$C_2H_4 + 3O_2 \rightarrow 2CO_2 + 2H_2O$$

One molecule of O_2 contains one O=O. One molecule of carbon dioxide contains two C=O bonds and one molecule of water contains two O–H bonds.

(a) State the number and type of each of the bonds from the table in one molecule of ethene. [2]
(b) Calculate the energy, in kJ, required to break the bonds in one molecule of ethene and three molecules of O_2. [1]
(c) Calculate the energy, in kJ, released when the bonds form in two molecules of carbon dioxide and two molecules of water. [1]
(d) Calculate the energy change, in kJ, for this reaction. [2]
(e) Explain whether the reaction is exothermic or endothermic based on your answer to **(d)**. [1]

4. Methane (CH_4) reacts with steam according to the balanced symbol equation:

$$CH_4(g) + 2H_2O(g) \rightarrow CO_2(g) + 4H_2(g)$$

(a) Use the bond energy values in the table below to calculate the energy change, in kJ, for the reaction. [4]

Bond	Bond energy (kJ)
H–H	436
C–H	412
O–H	463
C=O	803

(b) Explain whether the reaction is exothermic or endothermic, based on your answer to **(a)**. [1]

FURTHER CHEMICAL REACTIONS, RATES AND EQUILIBRIUM, CALCULATIONS AND ORGANIC CHEMISTRY

5. The diagram below shows the molecules involved in the reaction of hydrogen with oxygen.

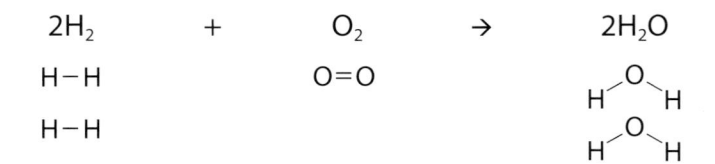

$$2H_2 + O_2 \rightarrow 2H_2O$$

H–H   O=O
H–H

The energy change for the reaction as shown above is –484 kJ.

(a) The bond energy of the H–H is 436 kJ and the bond energy for the O–H bond is 463 kJ. Calculate the bond energy of the O=O bond. [3]

(b) The reaction is exothermic. Explain, in terms of bonds, why the reaction is exothermic. [3]

6. A reaction profile for a reaction is given below.

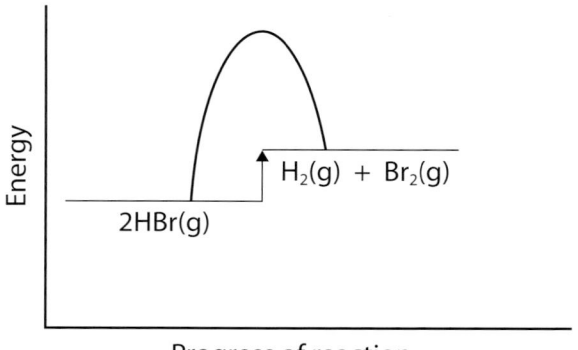

(a) Explain whether the reaction is exothermic or endothermic based on the reaction profile. [1]
(b) Label the activation energy on the reaction profile. [1]
(c) What is meant by activation energy? [1]
(d) Write a balanced symbol equation for the reaction including state symbols. [1]
(e) The bond energy values are H–Br = 362, H–H = 436 and Br–Br = 190. Calculate the energy change, in kJ, for this reaction. [4]

2.8 ENERGY CHANGES IN CHEMISTRY

7. The reaction below shows how hydrazine (N₂H₄) reacts with oxygen. Hydrazine is used as a rocket fuel.

$$N_2H_4 + O_2 \rightarrow N_2 + 2H_2O$$

The table below gives the bond energy values.

Bond	Bond energy (kJ)
N–H	386
N–N	163
N≡N	916
O–H	463
O=O	496

(a) Calculate the energy change, in kJ, for this reaction. [4]

(b) Complete the reaction profile shown below for reaction A showing the energy level of the products, the energy change and draw a reaction pathway labelling the activation energy. [4]

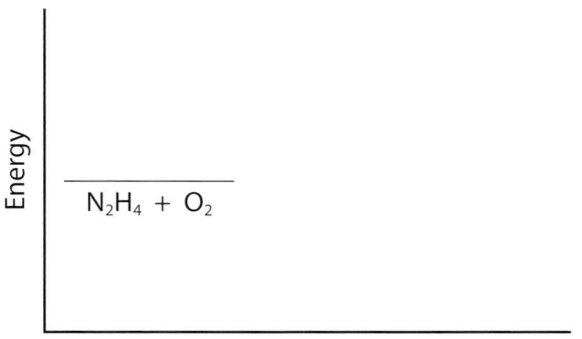

(c) Hydrazine decomposes into nitrogen and hydrogen and is seen as a potential source of hydrogen for use as a clean fuel. An iridium catalyst is used. The equation for the reaction is:

$$N_2H_4 \rightarrow N_2 + 2H_2$$

The energy change for the reaction is −81 kJ.

(i) The reaction is exothermic. Explain, in terms of bonds, why the reaction is exothermic. [3]

(ii) Calculate the bond energy of the H–H bond using the values in the table above and the energy change for the reaction. [4]

(iii) What is meant by the term catalyst? [2]

(iv) Explain how a catalyst increases the rate of a reaction. [2]

8. The reaction profile shown below is for the Haber process.

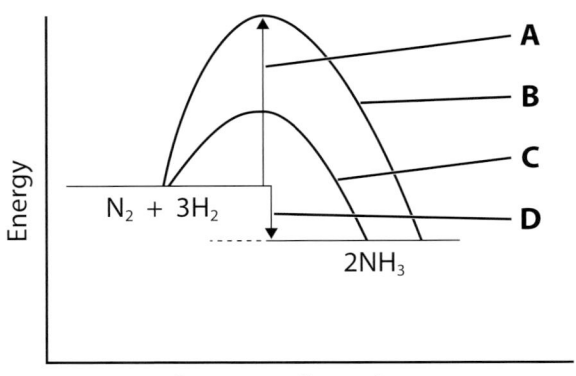

(a) Which letter (A, B, C or D) shows the reaction pathway for the catalysed reaction? [1]
(b) Which letter (A, B, C or D) shows the energy change for the reaction? [1]
(c) Which letter (A, B, C or D) shows the activation energy for the uncatalysed reaction? [1]
(d) Name the catalyst used in the Haber process. [1]
(e) The equation for the reaction is:

$$N_2 + 3H_2 \rightarrow 2NH_3$$

(i) The bond energy values are N≡N = 916 kJ, H−H = 436 kJ and N−H = 386 kJ. Calculate the energy change, in kJ, for the reaction. [4]
(ii) Explain whether the reaction is exothermic or endothermic. [1]

2.9 Gas Chemistry

1. Eight gases are listed below.

ammonia	carbon dioxide	chlorine	ethene
hydrogen	methane	oxygen	xenon

   (a) Which of the gases, if any, are coloured? [1]
   (b) Which of the gases may be prepared using calcium carbonate and hydrochloric acid? [1]
   (c) Which of the gases may be used as a clean fuel? [1]
   (d) Which of the gases is tested for using a glass rod dipped in concentrated hydrochloric acid? [1]
   (e) Which of the gases reacts with bromine water? [1]
   (f) Which of the gases is formed from the catalytic decomposition of hydrogen peroxide? [1]
   (g) If the relative formula mass (M_r) of a gas is greater than 30, the gas is denser than air. Which of the gases are denser than air? [1]

2. Nitrogen gas is found in the atmosphere and it is used in food packaging as it is an unreactive gas.

   (a) Explain why nitrogen is unreactive. [2]
   (b) State one other use of nitrogen gas. [1]
   (c) Complete the table below which details some of the gases found in the atmosphere, including nitrogen.

Gas	Percentage composition (%)
nitrogen	
	21
	0.037
argon	

   [4]

   (d) State two physical properties of nitrogen gas. [2]
   (e) The flowchart below shows how an impure sample of nitrogen could be prepared from air.

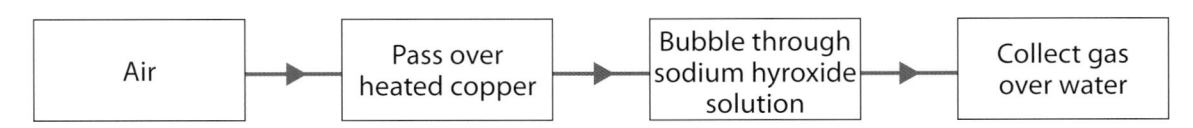

   Air → Pass over heated copper → Bubble through sodium hyroxide solution → Collect gas over water

   (i) State which gas in air would be removed by reacting with heated copper. [1]
   (ii) Which acidic gas in air would be removed by sodium hydroxide solution? [1]
   (iii) Name one gas, apart from nitrogen, which would remain in the collected gas. [1]

FURTHER CHEMICAL REACTIONS, RATES AND EQUILIBRIUM, CALCULATIONS AND ORGANIC CHEMISTRY

(f) Ammonia is manufactured from nitrogen and hydrogen in the Haber process.
  (i) Describe the test for ammonia gas. [3]
  (ii) Write a balanced symbol equation for the formation of ammonia from nitrogen and hydrogen. [3]
  (iii) State one use of ammonia. [1]

3. The apparatus shown below is used to prepare several gas jars of gases such as hydrogen, carbon dioxide and oxygen. A solid is placed in the conical flask and a solution added through the thistle funnel until the bottom of the thistle funnel is below the level of the solution in the flask.

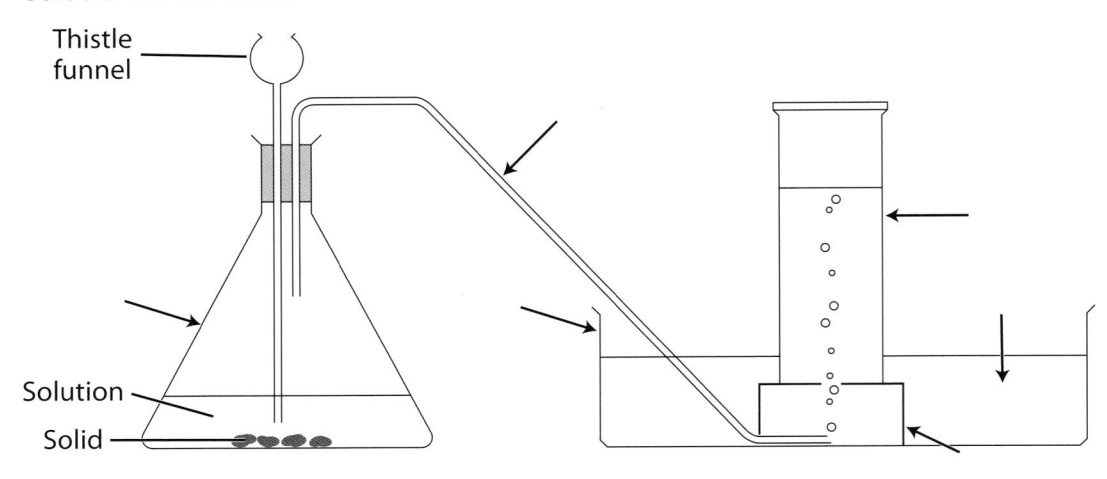

(a) Place each of the following labels on the diagram at the end of the appropriate arrow.

   conical flask   delivery tube   gas jar
   trough   water   beehive shelf
[6]

(b) Complete the table below with information about common gases and the solid and solution used to prepare the gases using the apparatus above.

Gas	Solid	Solution
	manganese(IV) oxide	
hydrogen		
	calcium carbonate	hydrochloric acid

[5]

(c) State two uses of hydrogen gas. [2]

(d) Explain why the bottom of the thistle funnel is below the level of the solution in the diagram. [1]

2.9 GAS CHEMISTRY

4. Sulfur reacts with oxygen according to the equation below:

$$S + O_2 \rightarrow SO_2$$

    (a) Name the product. [1]
    (b) Describe the appearance of sulfur. [2]
    (c) What is observed during the reaction? [2]
    (d) Describe the appearance of the product. [2]
    (e) Explain why sulfur is described as being oxidised in this reaction. [2]
    (f) 1.44 g of sulfur react with an excess of oxygen gas. Calculate the volume, in cm³, of SO_2 gas formed. [3]
    (g) 45 cm³ of SO_2, at 20 °C and 1 atm pressure, reacts with 0.15 mol/dm³ potassium hydroxide solution according to the equation:

$$SO_2(g) + 2KOH(aq) \rightarrow K_2SO_3(aq) + H_2O(l)$$

        (i) Calculate the number of moles of SO_2 in 45 cm³ at 20 °C and 1 atm pressure. [1]
        (ii) Calculate the number of moles of KOH which react with the sulfur dioxide. [1]
        (iii) Calculate the minimum volume of 0.15 mol/dm³ potassium hydroxide solution required to react with this volume of SO_2. [1]

5. Oxides are mostly basic or acidic.

    (a) Complete the table below to indicate if the oxides are basic or acidic by placing a tick (✓) in the appropriate column. One has been completed for you.

Oxide	Basic	Acidic
copper(II) oxide	✓	
sulfur dioxide		
magnesium oxide		
carbon dioxide		

[3]

    (b) Copper(II) oxide reacts with acids.

        (i) Write a balanced symbol equation for the reaction of copper(II) oxide with sulfuric acid. [2]
        (ii) What is colour change observed in the solution when copper(II) oxide reacts with sulfuric acid? [2]

FURTHER CHEMICAL REACTIONS, RATES AND EQUILIBRIUM, CALCULATIONS AND ORGANIC CHEMISTRY

6. Carbon dioxide is prepared by the reaction of calcium carbonate with hydrochloric acid.
   (a) Write a balanced symbol equation for the reaction of calcium carbonate with hydrochloric acid. [3]
   (b) Complete the diagram of the apparatus below to show how a gas jar of carbon dioxide would be collected over water. Label the diagram. [3]

   (Diagram: Thistle funnel, Conical flask, Hydrochloric acid, Calcium carbonate)

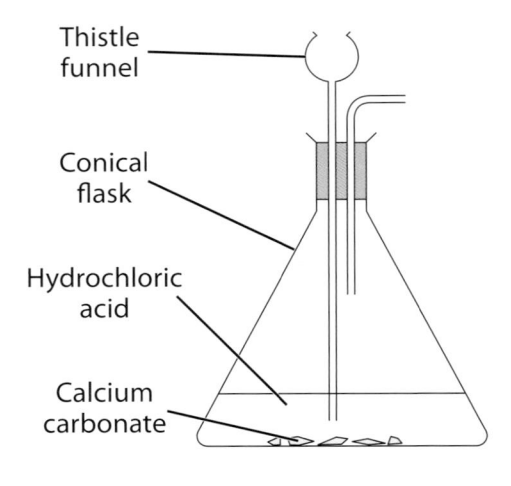

   (c) State two uses of carbon dioxide gas. [2]
   (d) Describe the test for carbon dioxide gas. [3]
   (e) 4.0 g of calcium carbonate were added to 50 cm³ of 2.0 mol/dm³ nitric acid (an excess). The equation for the reaction is:

   $$CaCO_3(s) + 2HNO_3(aq) \rightarrow Ca(NO_3)_2(aq) + CO_2(g) + H_2O(l)$$

   (i) Calculate the number of moles of calcium carbonate used. [1]
   (ii) Calculate the number of moles of carbon dioxide formed. [1]
   (iii) Calculate the volume, in dm³, of carbon dioxide formed at 20 °C and 1 atm pressure. [1]

7. Hydrogen peroxide solution decomposes in the presence of a catalyst to form oxygen gas and water. The equation for the reaction is:

   $$2H_2O_2(aq) \rightarrow 2H_2O(l) + O_2(g)$$

   (a) Name the catalyst used in the laboratory. [1]
   (b) Describe the appearance of the catalyst. [2]
   (c) 25.0 cm³ of 0.2 mol/dm³ hydrogen peroxide solution are completely decomposed.
       (i) Calculate the number of moles of hydrogen peroxide which reacts. [1]
       (ii) Calculate the number of moles of oxygen which is formed. [1]
       (iii) Calculate the volume, in cm³, of oxygen at 20 °C and 1 atm pressure which is formed. [1]

8. Carbon dioxide react with calcium hydroxide solution to form a milky white precipitate. When carbon dioxide is present in excess the milky white precipitate disappears.

    (a) What common name is used for calcium hydroxide solution? [1]

    (b) Write a balanced symbol equation for the reaction of carbon dioxide gas with calcium hydroxide solution. Include state symbols. [3]

    (c) Write a balanced symbol equation for the reaction of excess carbon dioxide with the milky white precipitate to form a colourless solution. [2]

9. Oxygen gas reacts with metallic and non–metallic elements.

    (a) Complete the table below.

Element	Name of the oxide	Formula of oxide
carbon		CO_2
magnesium	magnesium oxide	
copper		CuO

[3]

    (b) Write a balanced symbol equation for the reaction of magnesium with oxygen to form magnesium oxide. [3]

    (c) What is observed when magnesium reacts with oxygen? [3]

    (d) Magnesium oxide reacts with hydrochloric acid. Write a balanced symbol equation for the reaction. [3]

    (e) Carbon dioxide reacts with sodium hydroxide to form sodium carbonate and water. Write a balanced symbol equation for this reaction. [3]

    (f) Oxides may be described as basic or acidic. Classify each of the oxides in the table as basic or acidic. [1]

    (g) Name the product formed when CO_2 reacts with water. [1]

10. Hydrogen gas may be prepared using magnesium and hydrochloric acid or using zinc and hydrochloric acid. The reaction with zinc is safer as it is slower.

    (a) Explain, in terms of reactivity, why the reaction of zinc with hydrochloric acid is slower than the reaction of magnesium with hydrochloric acid. [2]

    (b) Write a balanced symbol equation for the reaction of zinc with hydrochloric acid. [3]

    (c) Explain why hydrogen may be described as a clean fuel. [2]

    (d) State two physical properties of hydrogen gas. [2]

    (e) Describe the test for hydrogen gas. [2]

Carbon dioxide gas is bubbled into three different solutions as shown in the diagram below.

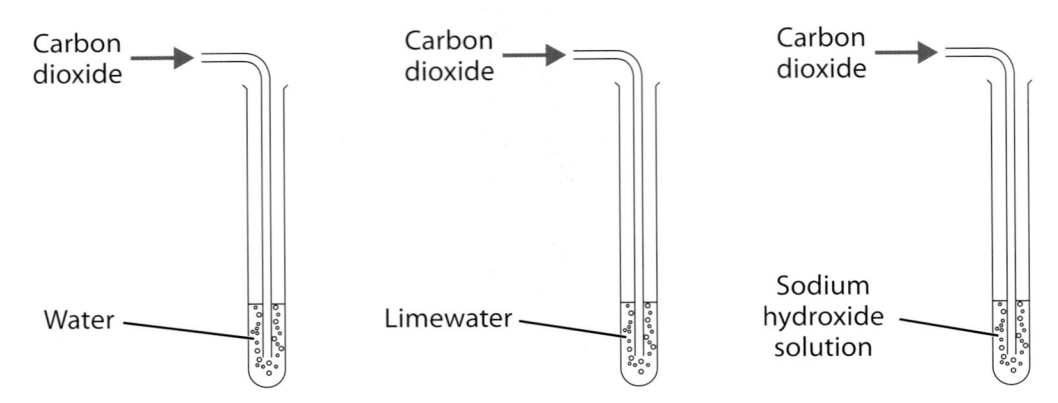

(a) Write a balanced symbol equation for the reaction of carbon dioxide with water and name the product. [3]
(b) What is the chemical name for limewater? [1]
(c) What is observed when carbon dioxide is bubbled into limewater until it is in excess? [3]
(d) Name the products of the reaction between carbon dioxide and sodium hydroxide solution. [2]
(e) Carbon dioxide is an acidic oxide.
   (i) Name one other acidic oxide. [1]
   (ii) Estimate the pH of a solution of carbon dioxide in water. [1]